EXTREME HYPNOTIC METHOD FOR WEIGHT LOSS

LEARN HOW TO CONTROL YOUR SUBCONSCIOUS MIND WITH HYPNOSIS TECHNIQUES, REGAIN YOUR SHAPE AND MAINTAIN HEALTHY HABITS

CARLA COMLEY

© **Copyright 2020 by Carla Comley - All rights reserved.**

The following Book is reproduced below with the goal of providing information that is as accurate and reliable as possible.

Regardless, purchasing this Book can be seen as consent to the fact that both the publisher and the author of this book are in no way experts on the topics discussed within and that any recommendations or suggestions that are made herein are for entertainment purposes only.

Professionals should be consulted as needed prior to undertaking any of the action endorsed herein.

This declaration is deemed fair and valid by both the American Bar Association and the Committee of Publishers Association and is legally binding throughout the United States.

Furthermore, the transmission, duplication, or reproduction of any of the following work including specific information will be considered an illegal act irrespective of if it is done electronically or in print.

This extends to creating a secondary or tertiary copy of the work or a recorded copy and is only allowed with the express written consent from the Publisher.

All additional right reserved.

The information in the following pages is broadly considered a truthful and accurate account of facts and as such, any inattention, use, or misuse of the information in question by the reader will render any resulting actions solely under their purview.

There are no scenarios in which the publisher or the original author of this work can be in any fashion deemed liable for any hardship or damages that may befall them after undertaking information described herein.

Additionally, the information in the following pages is intended only for informational purposes and should thus be thought of as universal.

As befitting its nature, it is presented without assurance regarding its prolonged validity or interim quality.

Trademarks that are mentioned are done without written consent and can in no way be considered an endorsement from the trademark holder.

TABLE OF CONTENTS

INTRODUCTION 8

HYPNOTHERAPY FOR WEIGHT LOSS, DOES IT WORK? 15

HYPNOSIS EXERCISE FOR WEIGHT LOSS 19

WEIGHT LOSS JOURNEY 26
- My Weight Loss Journey {How I Lost 100 Pounds} 28

HOW TO FALL INTO HYPNOSIS 36
- How to fall into hypnosis - The truth 36
- How To Fall Into Hypnosis - The truth (The Anti Hypnosis Clinic) 38

SELF-HYPNOSIS MOST RECOMMENDED TECHNIQUE 42
- Extreme rapid weight loss hypnosis for women - how does it work? 42
- How does hypnosis work? What is it about? 45
- How effective is hypnotherapy for weight loss? 46
- Build Affirmations to Maintain Healthy Habits 48

MAINTAINING WEIGHT LOSS 51
- How Does Rapid Weight Loss Hypnosis Work? 52
- The 17 Best Ways to Maintain Weight Loss 55

MOST EFFECTIVE AFFIRMATIONS TO LOSE WEIGHT – TOP 12 60

BENEFICIAL AFFIRMATION TO USE FOR WEIGHT LOSS 68
- What is extreme rapid weight loss hypnosis? 68
- Does extreme rapid weight loss hypnosis work? 68

TRAIN YOUR BRAIN TO LOVE EXERCISE 73
- Train your brain to love exercise and to eat healthily 73

EFFORTLESSLY BURN FAT 78
- Effortlessly burn fat without dieting. 78

INCREASE MOTIVATION 85

SELF-LOVE AND ACCEPTANCE 93

BENEFITS OF HYPNOSIS COMPARED TO RESTRICTED DIET 100

CONCLUSION 107

Introduction

It is no secret that people who exercise and eat right can live longer than those who do not. But which exercises are the best? What foods should you be eating more or less of to enjoy a long, healthy life? And what is the best way to ensure you adhere to these practices for many years down the line?

Find out in this book! We cover how important both diet and exercise are for longevity, as well as some specific things you need to keep an eye on if you want your physical health (and mental health) to last. Remember - a few minor changes now can lead to significant results in the future!

There's nothing better than investing in yourself. By now, most of you are well aware that health is of the utmost importance. That being said, it's always good to be reminded of the matter of investing in oneself. This is just as true when it comes to our bodies.

So, a few key points...

First, you need to know that exercise is essential for longevity - both physically and mentally. It can cause you to live longer and feel a lot better at the same time. A 2015 study, for example, found that exercise increases life expectancy by 4-10 years.

What's more, a study from the University of South Carolina and the US Department of Agriculture in 2007 showed that people who exercise regularly live longer than those who do not.

This goes for both men and women. Men who engage in moderate activity live seven years longer than those without any kind of physical activity - around 83 versus 68 years old. On the other hand, women benefit from increased life expectancy by 5-10 years if they exercise moderately - about 74 versus 66.

Fruits and vegetables are great for you...

No surprise here: fruits and vegetables are good for you! They contain vitamins and minerals that can help your body function properly. Simultaneously, people who eat plenty of fruits and vegetables tend to be healthier overall and live longer.

That's the reason why the World Health Organization suggests that adults should eat a minimum of 400 grams of fruit and vegetables a day.

If you are on the road to achieving this goal (which you should be!), make sure you try to include an assortment of different types of fruits and vegetables in your diet - at least five servings from each category a day. You also need to consume three servings from either the meat or dairy groups each day, so try to find something you like from both!

Another great thing about fruits and vegetables is that they provide your body with antioxidants - which help mitigate some free radical damage in your body. This is a bonus for you.

Fish, of course!

Again, no surprise here, but fish, in particular, have been shown to improve cardiovascular health and extend life expectancy. It's not just eating fish that helps you live longer - it's eating it regularly. Scientists discovered that it helps to reduce the risk of diabetes, heart disease, and other nasty diseases by as much as 40%!

However, there are a couple of issues with this one...

First of all: it's not always easy to determine which types of fish are healthy and not. This is because different types can be high in mercury or other toxins.

A few years ago, in a New England Journal of medicine, nine types of fish - which were commonly eaten in the US - were examined. They are all found to contain high levels of toxic chemicals that have been associated with some diseases. However, small amounts of mercury and other toxins are found in many types of fish - so you can't always rely on one test to show whether any particular fish is healthy or not.

Second: the benefits of fish are not known for every type. For instance, it has been found that eating herring can cause heart disease. However, there's no confirmation yet that that's true for all types of herring.

There is one method that does work, in any case. It's called the DASH Diet - short for Dietary Approaches to Stop Hypertension, which is a brilliant name in itself! The DASH diet is quick and to the point: it focuses on low sodium (sodium lowers blood pressure), fruits and vegetables (they're high in potassium), and lean protein.

It was created by researchers from the University of Miami in 1995 and has been proven very helpful in controlling hypertension.

The problem with "DASH" is that it's not very well known... A study from 2005 revealed that only 3% of people who lived below or above a certain threshold had ever heard of it.

We should all be eating more fish...

Fruits and vegetables are great, but you need to replace them with plenty of fish and other seafood. This is because getting enough protein is incredibly important for good health. It's just as important as the vitamins and minerals we get from fruits and vegetables.

A study published in the American Journal of Clinical Nutrition states that an increased intake of omega-three fatty acids combined with protein has been found to lower C-reactive protein levels (CRP) in healthy people. CRP is a marker for inflammation that can increase your risk of certain cancers or heart disease (and make you look older).

So go and start eating more fish! But make sure you're not overdoing it...

Too much tea is bad for you...

A study involving 1,972 people revealed that drinking tea regularly can be harmful to your health. Although green and black teas are generally very healthy, drinking too much of them will negate these benefits. The researchers conclude that if you drink four or more cups of green tea every day, you'll be at a higher risk of heart failure than those who drink none at all!

The scientists suggest that catechins - a type of antioxidant found in tea - can increase uric acid levels, damaging your kidneys. The source of the damage is unclear, but it's likely to be related to the amount of tea you drink.

Perhaps the most shocking finding was that even 2 cups of black tea a day were found to be linked with an increased risk of death, simply because they contained small amounts of green tea that was replacing them!

All in all, just one cup a day is fine, but if you're drinking more than that, then you're probably messing up your health. If you want an even healthier drink, try regular apple juice - it has no added sugar and is loaded with natural vitamins and antioxidants.

The best type?

You don't have to go out and buy expensive supplements or tablets to boost your levels. Many of the best vitamins and minerals are found in food.
An excellent way to get the most from your food is by juicing! Juicing is helpful because it enables you to extract the vitamins and minerals you need from foods rather than taking a pill. It

also cuts down on sugar intake and helps you lose weight and keep your body healthy, as described above.

Here's an example of a tasty juice that will give you everything you need: (The ingredients are shown in order of what's inside this drink - it doesn't matter which order they go in).

Asparagus and cucumber juice are great because they blend the vitamins and minerals of both asparagus and cucumber. For example, asparagus contains vitamin A which is good for your eyesight, teeth, bones, and skin, while cucumbers provide Vitamin C, which helps your immune system.

Tomato, carrot, and beetroot juice - sweet fruits like tomatoes are loaded with vitamins A, B6, and C. For example, a medium-sized tomato (they're usually sold in packs of 6 in supermarkets) provides 120% of your daily recommended intake of these three vitamins in just one serving! They also contain iron which is good for our bodies - especially for women who suffer from anemia.

Coconut water - a trendy beverage made quickly from coconut. Dieticians say you can drink 1000s of pints of this stuff every day without any adverse effects on your health!

Chia seeds are high in fiber, and even better, they're rich in omega six, which is good for our hearts and connective tissues. They also contain many minerals, including calcium, potassium, iron, and magnesium.

Herbal tea - tons of natural herbs mixed with hot water are widely available everywhere. This is one of the most popular drinks worldwide due to its numerous health benefits on the body and mind.

Lemon water - this is an excellent alternative to regular water due to the bright and refreshing taste. Served in a glass with ice cubes, it will cool you down on a hot day.

Hypnotherapy for Weight Loss, does it Work?

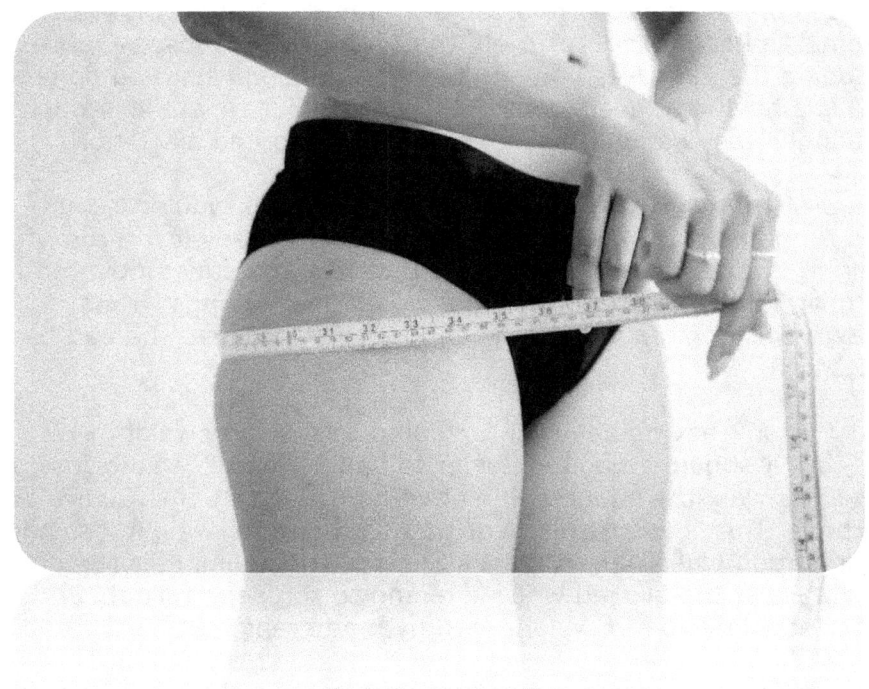

I've been weight-obsessed my entire life. I never felt as though I was beautiful, but that could've just been my perception of myself. Having low self-esteem is one thing, but having it so low that you feel like you need hypnosis for weight loss is another.

No matter what I did, nothing worked to keep me from being overweight and just not to like myself as a person. Hypnotherapy for weight loss was the only thing I had left to lose at this point because it worked on everyone else who tried it before me. So, I just gave it a shot.

I'm happy to say that I lost about 40 lbs. in my first month of hypnotherapy. I was thrilled with my results, but I had a few problems with my method.

First of all, it's tough to stay on track when you have nothing to lose. It doesn't matter how much weight you've already lost or how fast you need to lose it; if the exercises and diet are too hard for you to keep doing, then why would you start? That would make the situation much worse.

Instead of feeling too comfortable with my weight loss, I just needed to keep going. After all, the fastest way to lose weight is by doing the exercises you don't like and eating what you don't feel like having at every meal. My hypnosis for weight loss wasn't making it easy enough for me, so I needed to find a solution.

The assistant who came along with my hypnosis wouldn't even talk to me after a while, even though I had already lost a ton of weight. This assistant was supposed to help me stay motivated by giving me advice on how I was going about things wrong. I knew I was going about things bad, but not because she had told me so.

I just wasn't having any real fun doing this. Losing weight isn't fun, but it should be a little easier to handle than it was for me. I felt like I was just on a bland diet without any actual structure or purpose. This is what I felt like; that hypnosis for weight loss had no intention when all you do is sit in front of a computer screen and stare at the ground while listening to someone talk about other people who lost weight with hypnotherapy.

When you know how to use hypnotherapy for weight loss, it's not all that hard to do. I can't even count how many times my assistant tried to tell me that I was doing it wrong and that there were other things I should try, like meditation. Again, this is just a distraction from what the main goal is with hypnosis.

If you don't have the right way of using hypnotherapy for weight loss, then you're probably never going to lose any weight, no matter what your goals are. You'll make yourself miserable and finish up by giving up on the whole process altogether. I knew that I needed to use hypnosis in a more effective way than I had been, but it just didn't seem to be working.

Why did weight loss fail for me? Why was I constantly failing at losing weight no matter what I did? Then, it finally hit me. It wasn't that my method wasn't working; it was because nobody else had ever tried this hypnosis for weight loss before me. No one had ever used this method of losing weight before, so there was no natural way of measuring whether or not it worked or not.

If you want to lose weight, then you need to learn to use hypnotherapy. If you don't, then it's just going to be a part of your life that you hate and think is pointless. I had tried other methods of losing weight before, but they were all too hard for me. None worked fast enough, and none worked long enough for me actually to lose the weight I needed to lose.

Hypnosis is the answer! It requires a lot of hard work, but it will be worth it when the process is complete because it will work faster than any other method of losing weight that has ever been used before. Hypnosis is the future, and I'm proud to be a part of it.

Hypnosis Exercise for Weight Loss

Hypnosis exercise for weight loss is an effective way to lose weight fast and maintain weight loss. It works well for men and women who are motivated, have a strong desire for the change in their body and mind, improves their self-image, and are willing to work hard on themselves.

Hypnosis is different from so-called quick-fix techniques like diet pills or fad diets. If you're going to do hypnosis exercise for weight loss, you need to commit yourself fully or not bother at all.

When you listen to the hypnosis tapes for weight loss, you are in a relaxed state. Hypnosis allows your subconscious mind to work more efficiently and faster by using more attention to the task at hand. It helps you achieve your goals much quicker than if you were going through it on your own. You can get a much better result in about two weeks with hypnosis exercise than if you were taking time off from your usual exercise routine for your body to get used to the new changes and gain some necessary weight loss momentum.

Maintaining and achieving weight loss success with hypnosis exercise is much easier than it is without hypnosis. The hypnosis enables you to condition your mind to react to how you want it to respond to food and the desire to eat. You can put yourself in a stronger position concerning food and eating for life without burdening yourself with too many rules that you would eventually find difficult or impossible to follow.

Hypnosis exercise for weight loss gives you the strength and fortitude you need when your willpower is not enough. Using self-hypnosis exercise, you won't have all the self-doubt or fear of failure before starting on a new diet plan or exercise program. The hypnosis will help give you exactly what it takes for your body weight to be standard throughout your lifetime.

No wonder hypnosis for weight loss is so popular. Not only the hypnosis exercise can help you to lose weight fast, but it also allows you to keep your weight off. All of us want that nice, healthy, attractive body and don't want the heartache of regaining every ounce of it when we diet.

During your life, there are times when you may be in a situation that makes it difficult for you to exercise. This could happen because of a hectic work schedule or an injury that prevents you from doing regular exercise. These are reasons why many people gain their weight back once they're finished dieting and start exercising again. You can avoid weight gain if you follow the directions of an exercise program. However, if your schedule does not permit you to exercise regularly, try one of the following solutions:
Take care of your body and health by eating healthy food and keeping pace with your daily routine. Make it a habit to exercise at least 30 minutes daily. An excellent way to exercise is by using a home exercise machine or doing sit-ups or push-ups on your hand. If you cannot afford an expensive home gym, purchase a small set for yourself that includes an elliptical trainer, a treadmill, and some other essential items that make getting in shape more accessible than it would be otherwise.

Don't watch television if you're not able to exercise during the day. Watching too much television can cause your metabolism to slow down. You will have to take care of your body and health beyond dieting, so make sure that you don't spend too much time in front of the television.

Schedule some time for exercise. Even though this might not be enough time for a regular workout, at least you are getting some benefits from exercise that you can build on over time. Even 10 minutes of exercise a day is better than nothing at all.
Eat healthy food while dieting so that your body can get the nutrition it needs to hold on to any weight loss gained during daily exercises or regular workouts.

It is essential to do your research in advance before you choose a home exercise machine. The one you choose must be the right one for your needs and conditions. A few options such as treadmills, stationary bicycles, cross trainers will need some space around them to be adjusted when needed. Also, don't forget that the length required will depend on how many people begin to use them simultaneously and how they're going to do their exercises. So make sure that you have plenty of space all around, or else you might not get your money's worth.

As with all plans for weight loss, getting started may take some time and patience. But the key to maintaining your new weight, reducing your risks of chronic health problems, and enjoying the life you've always wanted is to use your home exercise machine regularly. The benefits gained from a healthy diet and regular exercise are worth the effort and time you put in.

You should never participate in any home fitness equipment that you can't afford to replace. If you have a good reason for the purchase, explain it to your family and friends and tell them that they're helping you keep fit.
One of the best ways to lose weight is to eat healthily. Here are some tips from the Mayo Clinic on how you can lose weight:

It's been said that a healthy diet and regular exercise are the keys to success with dieting. This is true, but there are other factors that you may not have considered. One of these factors is your man's personality. The subject of men and food is so broad that it would be impossible for me to cover it in any kind of detail. The answer to the question I posed in the title is simple: Men are different from women when it comes to dieting.

The first thing men learn when they start dieting is that they can't eat anything they want anymore. They have to watch what they're eating and then watch the calories burned by exercise.

Dieting can be a great challenge for men because most don't like seeing themselves as dimwits or as losers incapable of doing anything right. However, these feelings will only last until your husband sees results from his efforts with dieting.

When your husband begins to see results, he will feel better about himself and start looking forward to his new body and lifestyle. He might also feel closer to you if you are also dieting. This is a good thing because it means your husband will be more likely to stick with his diet long enough to get the results he's after.

When men begin their diets, they often have a lot of weight to lose. The more weight they need to lose, the harder it is for them to keep their food intake under control. This is because they may not believe they'll be successful with their diets and will tend to do things that sabotage their efforts.

The important thing you can do when your husband starts losing weight is supported him. Try to encourage him when he needs it and be supportive when he has doubts about the way his diet is going. Your husband's support will make all the difference as he struggles with weight loss.

Research shows that obese people tend to get less satisfaction from eating than those of average weight do. This may be because they have to eat a lot more to get the same satisfaction as someone who isn't overweight.

Recipes for successful dieting include eating more protein and fiber-rich foods and drinking plenty of water. The most important thing you can do is make sure your husband eats a healthy breakfast to get him started right. In the long run, this will help keep him from cheating on his diet or eating larger meals than he needs to.

There are many things you should know about men and diets, but you've already learned enough to make your husband's weight loss an enjoyable experience for both of you.

You can begin to help your husband when he decides to diet by encouraging him and being a source of support for him. If you can do this, he'll be more likely to lose weight and keep it off.

If your husband decides to start dieting, the best thing you can do is be supportive. As his wife, you have the power to help him and make his weight loss success. Dieting isn't easy, but with your support, your husband's chances of losing weight are much greater than if he tried to do it alone.

Healthcare providers may ask you some questions when your husband visits them for a check-up. He may be asked to undergo specific tests to find out if he has diabetes.
A urine test is one of the tests your husband's doctor may give him. If blood glucose levels are abnormal, this is indicated by a positive result. A sample should be taken after your husband has been fasting for 12 hours. If the test is positive, another test (glucose tolerance test) will confirm the finding.

If your husband's doctor thinks that he may have diabetes, they'll usually recommend that he visit a diabetologist to diagnose and treat diabetes. Your husband will probably have some more tests before he's diagnosed with diabetes – these are usually done in a hospital setting. In some cases, he may also have an oral glucose tolerance test that involves drinking a sugary liquid.

Diabetes is a disease in which you have an elevated blood glucose level. This could be because your body doesn't process sugars properly and can't convert sugar and other carbohydrates into energy. In some cases, type-2 diabetes is also associated with obesity, high cholesterol levels, and high blood pressure.

The treatment for diabetes includes diet changes and exercise, pills to help regulate blood glucose levels, insulin injections or insulin therapy for people with Type 1 diabetes (insulin), and the use of foot care and other aids. Diabetes can affect various organ systems in your body, such as your eyes, feet, kidneys, heart, or nerves. All these organs can be affected by diabetes, so you must take care of your health to prevent organ damage or failure.

Diabetes is a significant disease that must be treated because it can cause various health problems if left untreated. As a spouse, you are the best person to monitor and help your husband with his treatment. It's up to you as his spouse and partner to make sure that he follows his doctor's recommendations and keeps himself healthy.

Weight Loss Journey

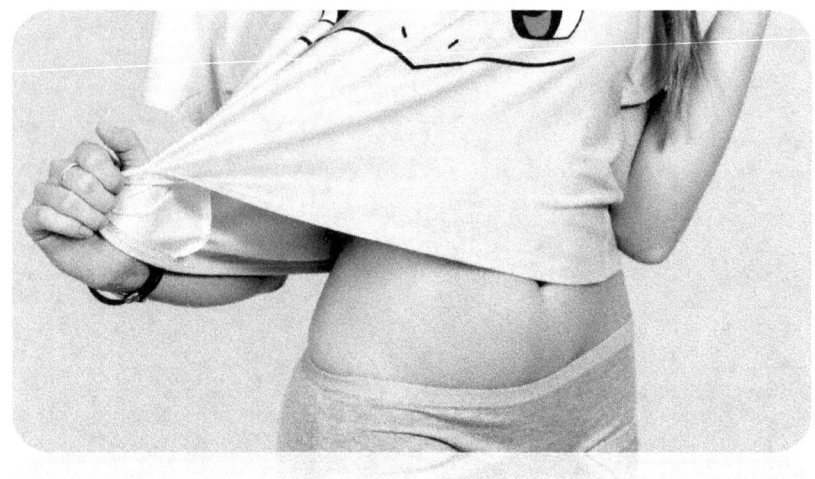

The weight loss journey is not an easy path to take. It's a huge uphill battle that starts with the mind. You have to learn how to be confident in yourself and your body to have a healthy transformation. Luckily, hypnosis is here.

Hypnosis is an excellent way of healing the mind because when you're focused on something else, you can't dwell on all of your negative thoughts and worries that are ruining your day-to-day life. So it's an excellent way to get started on your new weight loss regimen.

The best time to start the hypnosis is in the morning because you will be focused and can learn your new habits with ease.

To begin, find a quiet place where you can relax and focus on yourself. Make sure no one interrupts your session or distracts you because this might ruin the whole process.

Once you're ready, the journey can begin. You'll feel comfortable and prepared to get to know your new body.

You may feel a bit strange at first, but you'll only be in this state for a couple of minutes, so it's not much of a problem. You can also go with hypnosis before bed and wake up feeling refreshed and ready to start the day.

Step 1: The induction phase is when you will be guided into hypnosis with techniques such as visualization exercises, guided imagery, and self-hypnosis.
Step 2: The second phase is when your subconscious mind will be given instructions to eliminate all the negative feelings regarding your body.

Step 3: The final phase is when you will be guided into a state of deep relaxation so that your body can remove all negative energy and accept a new, healthier personality.
To lose weight through hypnosis, you must be willing to give it everything you have and do whatever it takes to see results, even if it means following a strict diet made, especially for you by your doctor. This will ensure results and not just weight loss; staying fit.

I guarantee you will follow through with this process because it will be easy, and you'll have a new body that fits your lifestyle now. It's the easiest way to get rid of bad habits and start a new you.
The process is straightforward because it is s subjective method and can be used by anyone. You just have to follow these steps. Remember, "you do not need extreme weight loss hypnosis for women; you just need a little help."

My Weight Loss Journey {How I Lost 100 Pounds}

"Today, I'm 100 pounds lighter than I was the point at which I began my weight reduction venture."

My story isn't one of the overnight achievements. I didn't take a sorcery pill. My outcomes were not from a craze diet or an item from an infomercial. My excursion has been more similar to a crazy ride of preliminaries, numerous mistakes, and an assortment of little achievements en route, in the end prompting more than I at any point expected to acquire.

I was a sad young lady with no confidence, caught underneath a loose shirt and stretchy pants and urgent to get in shape to be typical simply. I had no clue that it would transform into an excursion of self-disclosure, opportunity, and discovering delight. Gracious no doubt, and 100-pound weight reduction.

Diets I Tried on My Weight Loss Journey

Over numerous long stretches of attempting to get thinner, I tried various weight reduction diets, programs, and surprisingly a few tricks.

I wish I had been contributing to a blog while I'd been on every one of them. However, I attempted many of them when I was very youthful, so there is no put-down account of my experience. Here are just a few of the many things I tried:
Slim-Fast
Atkins
Juicing
The Whole 30
weight loss pills
Weight Watchers
ab belts
stomach shrinking wraps
calorie counting
skipping meals

Growing Up As The Fat Kid

I was a cute kid. A cute kid (that's me being cute in between my two older sisters in the picture below)....until 1st grade. I don't have the foggiest idea why I began gorging in any case.

I was possible because I was a daddy's young lady, and I needed to stay aware of his bits to be very much like him.
Conceivably, I was obstinate and realized my mom needed to eat vigorously, so I revolted by sneaking lousy nourishment.

Maybe I super cherished food (and still do!). On the day after I was conceived, my mother expressed, "It seems like you simply need to eat ALL the time!" <-Yup.
Whatever the explanation, I began gorging and just couldn't stop.
I recollect my grandma saying something once about how stunned she was that I could eat countless such cuts of pizza.

What's more, I felt pleased with having the option to do as such. I adored lousy nourishment and would sneak into the kitchen late around evening time and discover the unhealthiest food my mother had stowing away in the kitchen… and I'd eat everything at a time.

Regardless of whether it was a case of Nutty Bars, a sack of chips, or some genuinely flavorful extras, I'd eat them up.

Food (all the more explicitly, shoddy nourishment) was a valuable item to me. When it was there, I inclined that it was an asset that could run out at some random time, so I needed to eat everything as quick as conceivable before another person set out to attempt it themselves and leave less for me.

I was practically similar to Joey from Friends. "Becky doesn't share food!"
Dislike I was at any point denied.

My mom was (and still is) a phenomenal cook. She generally made a huge load of tasty, sound, natively constructed suppers; however, I never valued them.
I was continually asking for prepared food varieties, prepackaged food sources, and cheap food.

I would have taken a Lunchable over a sandwich quickly and wished I could live off doughnuts, potato toddlers, and cupcakes.

I strikingly recall wishing somebody would supplant all drinking fountains with Kool-Aid wellsprings (fun actuality – I didn't begin loving plain water until I was 27 years of age).

The Opposite Extreme

That year, I became hopelessly enamored.
We dated, we got ready for marriage, and afterward, he was sent, and I lived in a steady condition of pressure.

I floated to the next outrageous of undesirable weight reduction. I was hopeless. I thought stressing was the solitary thing I could offer by then, and since I was unable to control what was happening abroad, I chose to control my eating. I was living alone and, for most of that year, I presumably ate between 500-800 calories every day.

I was ravenous a great deal, not practicing by any means, had no energy, and my stomach was continually in tangles, yet I shed 40 pounds, bringing me down to 160. That was the lightest I'd been since I could recall (in an absolute sense. I needed to have been 160 pounds sooner or later in my life as I was putting on the weight. However, I have no clue about when that was).

I thought thin implied sound, yet even though I was, at last, a typical weight, I was FAR from solid by then.

Unfortunate Relationship, Unhealthy Body

The arrangement finished, he returned home, and we got hitched. I was prepared for a delighted particular first-night stage. However, it was anything but a glad or a good marriage.

I didn't have any acquaintance with it at that point. Yet, my profound instabilities from being the fat child blended in with that urgency for consideration from folks had driven me into a sincerely oppressive marriage.

My weight reduction venture spiraled down, and my weight shot up indeed.

We a ton of cheap food, once in a while practiced because we were stuck to our TV and PC screens, and the pressure of the constant clash between us was almost terrible (particularly for this human satisfying, harmony adoring young lady!), so I began recovering the weight rapidly.

And afterward, I continued acquiring.
Furthermore, acquiring.
Until January 2012. I was 194 pounds and was scared of crawling back up into the 200's.

I began purchasing more modest garments and seeing that things fit me such a ton better, yet it was brief.
I'll Exercise... In Secret.
In this way, I joined a rec center.

I was honestly just happy with utilizing the curved. I was too frightened to even think about attempting any of the classes offered, and the weight machines were simply scary. Rec center individuals consistently appear to understand what they're doing and I just... didn't.

I didn't feel like I fit anyplace. I particularly didn't need individuals to see my exercise center insufficiency, so I invested a ton of energy in the cardio film room, where the entirety of the lights is diminished. They projected motion pictures onto a screen before the cardio gear.

I attempted a fitness coach for a spell and hated it.
An individual watching me practice was. The. Most noticeably awful.
Generally, because I was frail to such an extent that I battled with a ton of the activities she gave me and however sweet as this young lady might have been, she consistently communicated how shocked she was at how little I could lift/push/squat/whatever else. Even though I was 55 pounds, not precisely my heaviest, I felt deficient and needed to stow away.
That is the point at which I chose to begin running.
Indeed, running.

My weight loss journey has been so much bigger than 100 pounds

It gave me freedom and such deep joy.

I learned to trade my guilt for God's grace.
It improved my relationships.
I feel so much better.
It boosted my confidence.
I learned how to find joy and satisfaction in self-control.
I improved my relationship with God and others.
It changed my life into one that I am madly in love with living.
And now, I need to give that to other people. I need you to realize that, regardless of what your beginning spot is, you can find that opportunity, as well.
As a supporter of Christ, you have the force of God on your side, so regardless of how incomprehensible or sad your circumstance appears, I can guarantee you there is a universe of expectation and probability sitting tight for you.
At times you simply need somebody to have faith in you and help you venture out.

You can lose weight and carry on with a better life, regardless of the distance away you feel from that objective at this moment. One stage, each little change, in turn, changes your life.

You can do this!

How to Fall into Hypnosis

How to fall into hypnosis - The truth

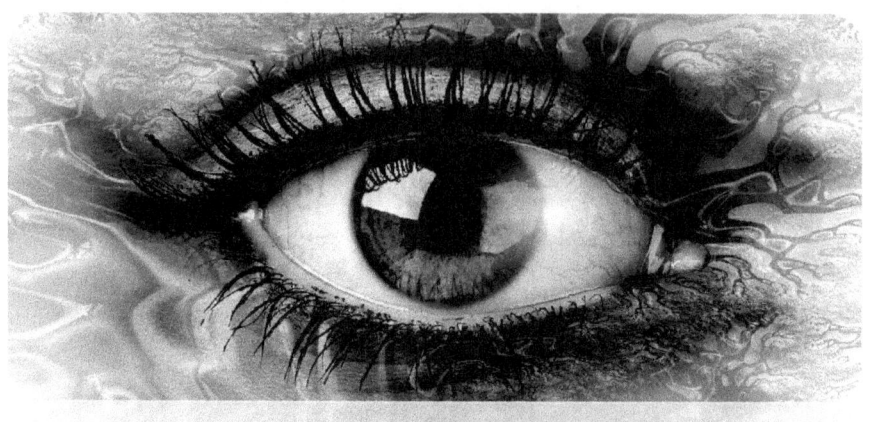

Do you think you probably have a pretty good idea of how hypnosis works? To put it simply, people under the influence of hypnosis can be immersed in an artificially induced waking dream. They lose their connection to reality and are focused on what's happening inside their head, but they continue moving about in a trance-like state.

A few years ago, I went through the process of breaking up with my boyfriend. It was challenging, and I didn't know how to cope with it. Out of desperation, I took the advice from someone who told me that this "extreme rapid weight loss hypnosis for women" was just what I needed to get over him quickly. I was on board and went to his house to get it done.

When I got there, he put me through the whole process, which involved being in a trance for about an hour and labeling my thoughts one by one. For example, if I thought of him, I had to say "past" out loud. It was pretty easy, and I didn't have any trouble getting myself into or out of hypnosis. He told me how all that was left to do after that would be repeating some affirmations he gave me over and over again whenever I felt sad or alone.

That is when my problems started. I couldn't stop thinking about him and how great he was. I would repeat the affirmations whenever I remembered, but it didn't seem to be helping. It only made me think about her more. Then I realized that he had been in on this whole thing from the beginning and had just wanted my money to try out some new hypnosis techniques on me!

So what is the truth? It's not so much about what you can do with hypnosis as it knows who you are dealing with and their agenda. Some people have a genuine interest in helping others, but other people will take advantage of anyone they can.

The problem is that the person under hypnosis seems to be completely unaware of what's going on. I can tell you right now that the affirmations are a waste of time!

Excerpt: 'HOW TO FALL INTO HYPNOSIS'

How To Fall Into Hypnosis - The truth (The Anti Hypnosis Clinic)

'HOW TO FALL INTO HYPNOSIS'...without even knowing it... This article will explain the truth about hypnosis, and it will also allow you to discover a way to fall under hypnosis without even knowing it.

You might even ask yourself, "What is hypnosis?" Hypnosis is the process by which you can change your thoughts. It's when you're so caught up in what is happening inside your head that nothing else seems to matter. But what exactly is this process? How does it work? How do you get there? What can you expect while you are under hypnosis? To answer all of these questions, I will take a look at the three stages of hypnosis, and then we will touch on one way that you might be able to fall into a real trance without even knowing it.

I will also give you a few tips on using this method to relax and fall into hypnosis. There were times when I wanted to fall under hypnosis so badly, but I just couldn't do it. A friend of mine said that she had something that would help me put me at ease, and she recommended that I listen to the recording. After hearing this tape, I wanted to know if it would work for me, but then again, what was there to know? It's all in your head anyway! Hypnosis has gotten a bad rap in recent years, no doubt because of the way that some people have used it.

They've ditched the hypnosis, and they've decided to give up on the idea of trying to use it. Some people think that everyone in the world is a hypnotherapist, and if you're not a professional hypnotist, you're stuck with nothing. Well, I can tell you right now that this is not true at all. If you are having trouble using hypnosis on your friends or family members to help them with their problems, you are doing other things wrong. For instance:

1) You might be using the wrong techniques for hypnotizing them.....

2) You might be forgetting to mention what will happen while your subject is hypnotized...

3) You might be underestimating the ability of the subject to recover from the suggestions that you make...

4) Your voice might have a "lack of projection" quality, making it difficult for people to listen to you...

5) Maybe you are just not a good enough hypnotist yet, and that's why your subjects won't listen to you. You need more practice! Well, if this is true, then hypnosis is nothing at all like most people believe. People think that hypnosis is some mystical power they have, but it's completely different in reality. Hypnosis is nothing more than a state of focus. If you can get someone to focus entirely on you and your suggestions, then they will almost instantly find themselves in a hypnotic trance.
The key is to make sure that your tips are interesting enough for the person to want to focus on them. It's simple to make sure that you know what your subject wants most, and then give it to them! If a person does not understand how hypnosis works, they are just going to create problems for themselves.

They are going to confuse hypnosis with anything else that they can find. They will use words like "trance" and "trancelike" when they mean that they are not getting any results. They will wonder why they aren't gaining the products they want, and then they will give up on hypnosis altogether. If this happens, then you can pretty much forget about trying to hypnotize them; because it just will never work!

The subject cannot be hypnotized if their mind has already been made up against hypnosis. You must convince them of the benefits of using hypnosis by showing your issue exactly how useful it can be for them...If you can do this, then you should have no trouble at all! It's interesting that as soon as they begin to understand precisely what a hypnotic trance is and exactly how it works; then they usually find themselves in one of these trances almost instantly. I guess that this is just the way it is.

The subject will be ready with their mind when you are ready with the suggestions. If you are not prepared, then you will find yourself waiting and waiting and waiting some more... You want to make sure that your subject understands hypnosis better than the average person does.

This way, they will have no problem getting into a hypnotic trance. It's hard to explain exactly how hypnosis works. So I usually stick with the basics for the time being. After someone understands what magic is, they are generally good to go! It's interesting to note that when a subject is in a hypnotic trance... I find myself moving through the motions that I am going to use as I go along.

Like I said before, I don't always follow all of my suggestions. For instance, sometimes, when I'm speaking about something that I'm not too sure about, the subject will stop me right there and ask me what it is that they are supposed to be doing or saying...

It's funny how things like this happen. But this has happened more than once! There are times where the subject becomes so intent on what they are doing... then the suggestion just slips by them on its own! The point here is that your recommendations should always be relevant.

Self-Hypnosis Most Recommended Technique

Self-hypnosis most recommended rapid weight loss safe technique for women. Hypnosis is a natural way to lose weight without the need for gimmicks, pills, or fad diets. The subconscious mind has a great deal more power and influence over us than many people realize. Reconnect with this power through hypnosis, and you will no longer be a slave to food!

Extreme rapid weight loss hypnosis for women - how does it work?

Hypnosis relies on the innate ability of our subconscious minds to create change in our lives by making positive suggestions that over time become more accessible and easier to follow as they sink deeper into your psyche with every passing day.

You are in control of your weight and size, not the world or the food industry. The good news is that you can use your mind to make these changes easy and fast. It works by helping you eliminate the old patterns that have held you back.

Instead of eating like a crazy person or lacking self-control, hypnosis helps you make peace with yourself and with food. You can finally learn to listen to your body's needs and develop healthy habits and attitudes toward eating as well as exercise. You can take charge of your body and life and use your mind to guide you to the wonderful woman you want to be, and the experience of weight loss is the reward.

You have been given a key that unlocks a door that has been locked for far too long. Permit yourself to let go of your past and embrace this new life. Don't wait any longer - it's time for weight loss hypnosis!

What are the benefits?

Hypnotism provides a safe and straightforward approach to lose weight and keep it off. You will get rid of all bad eating habits that lead to long-term health problems. The use of hypnosis makes quick weight loss possible, as it is a natural way.

How to start?

For fast and pleasant weight loss, you need to begin with small changes on your part, which will lead you to changes in your life that you never thought possible.

You will learn a new way to think about food, eating habits, and exercise.

You will come to enjoy the inner freedom that comes with weight loss and self-hypnosis. You can do this! It is not difficult if you follow the suggestions given below:

Breathe deeply and relax: Make yourself comfortable, sit up straight in an armchair or lie down on your bed. Relax and just breathe deeply into your stomach as if it were a balloon. Count backward from 10 to 1, letting your breathing slow as you go down every number. Use the power of focus - Close your eyes, and use all of your senses to experience this new feeling fully. It's easy to get distracted by the thoughts that bombard your mind, but you have to push these away and keep your ideas simple. Positive affirmations - You must tell yourself that you are eating healthy food and are moving more because you want to be strong and active.

These words must go deep into your subconscious mind. Be careful with the negative words such as don't or no. You can try eating an apple a day for lunch at work. A mix between hypnosis sessions, exercise, and some healthy meal replacements like smoothies in a blender. You will be surprised when you see the result.

Self-hypnosis for ultimate weight loss is a natural way to lose weight quickly and easily. The biggest reason why it works is that it encourages positive thinking. If you are more optimistic, you will stick to your diet and the exercises that you learned from hypnosis sessions. With hypnosis, you can expect to feel better, have more energy, and lose the weight that has been bothering you all these years. Give it a try today!
Your subconscious mind has a lot of power over your body's state of health and ability to lose weight fast. You can get rid of bad habits and work on creating a positive, healthy attitude toward food.

How does hypnosis work? What is it about?

Hypnosis is a state in which people experience heightened concentration and increased receptiveness to suggestions. Hypnosis may be used for different purposes (including treatment of pain). Hypnotherapy is usually used by psychotherapists who specialize in this area. However, many self-help guides help people use self-hypnosis for their purpose.

What are the benefits of hypnosis?

Maintaining an attitude of positive expectation should help you to lose weight. Only by practicing this type of thinking, positive changes can be made in your life. You will be more confident and happy because you will give up harmful habits that cause you to feel less than healthy. The hypnotist will help you with the process by giving you easy-to-follow suggestions that may include affirmations and suggestions about healthy eating, exercise, and other positive ideas to encourage a healthier lifestyle.

How effective is hypnotherapy for weight loss?

The effectiveness of any type of treatment depends mainly on the psychological willingness and motivation of the patient. The hypnotist will explain to you (and your partner if you are working together) the entire process ahead of time. Taking home a video to watch as a couple will help your partner understand the psychotherapy and aid in his or her support for your efforts. Only by practicing this type of thinking, positive changes can be made in your life. You will be more confident and happier because you will give up harmful habits that cause you to feel less than healthy. The hypnotist will help you with the process by giving you easy-to-follow suggestions that may include affirmations and suggestions about healthy eating, exercise, and other positive ideas to encourage a healthier lifestyle.

Hypnotherapy is better than any alternative because you get the psychological help, support, encouragement, and ongoing guidance that we provide as part of our service. Hypnosis can be used to encourage weight loss in people of all ages. It is very effective for people who are overweight or obese. However, since hypnosis is not a medical procedure, it will not eliminate medical issues that might require medical intervention.

Hypnosis is based on the principle that we have a subconscious mind and a conscious mind. The subconscious mind is the part of our brain that makes decisions about life's most important things, such as love, health, and money. Hypnosis is based on helping the patient learn to control their inner world via the conscious mind.

Hypnotherapy helps you reach goals more efficiently than any other therapy because you get the psychological help, support, encouragement, and ongoing guidance that we provide as part of our service.

Hypnosis can be used to encourage weight loss in people of all ages. It is very effective for people who are overweight or obese. Hypnotherapy can be used in several ways to reduce and help people stop smoking. It is effective when used as part of a weight loss program or when assisting people to quit drinking. It is also suitable for overcoming or preventing stress and anxiety. Hypnotherapy can help with phobias, chronic pain, relaxation, self-esteem, and many other psychological issues that can be co-morbidities with weight issues.

Build Affirmations to Maintain Healthy Habits

1. "I am in control. I make the decisions about what I eat and when I work out."
2. "I am always patient and willing to take on any challenge put in front of me."
3. "No one else decides for me, but me."
4. "I love to eat well-balanced meals and get plenty of rest each day."
5. "I am confident that my body is a beautiful machine that will always respond with grace when it's given the proper care."
6. "I can read my body and its signals."
7. "My body is always telling me what it needs to succeed."
8. "I am disciplined and have high self-esteem."
9. "I love to be active."
10. "My workouts are fun and challenging."
11. "My nutrition is wholesome."

Gain Confidence from Great Results!

1. Develop a plan for food preparation based on the four food groups: protein, carbohydrate, fat, and vegetable/fruit servings (5 servings). Purchasing meals with the proper nutritional value helps you stay on track. Know the serving sizes of all foods so that you can visualize appropriate portions.

2. Create a menu with foods from each of the four food groups and take it with you when you go shopping.

3. Avoid processed foods, which are often high in sugar, sodium, and saturated fat.

4. Do not skip meals! Hunger pangs lead to cravings that often result in overeating or snacking on unhealthy foods. Try to eat small portions throughout the day instead of three large meals to avoid high blood sugar levels and unnecessary snacking between meals.

5. Keep a food diary for at least one month to help identify what triggers your eating habits (such as stress).

6. Be aware that aroma impacts appetite. Keep tempting foods out of the house!

7. For a long-term solution to weight gain, consider your activity level. If it is low, set small-scale goals (such as walking 10 minutes a day three times per week) and be sure to reward yourself for your progress!
Perfect Your Posture

1. Perfect posture will come naturally with the use of mirror therapy (the study of self-image). When you learn to love looking at yourself in the mirror, you will become more aware of how you stand and sit for more extended periods so that you can improve your posture.

2. If you are not used to having good posture, you may feel out of place when standing, walking, or sitting up straight. To work on this area of your life, make an effort to correct your posture as soon as you feel off balance. Become aware of your body and its actions in a mirror or while someone is watching.

3. If you are standing or sitting up comfortably with good posture, visualize yourself with poor posture and try to aim for better positioning immediately!

4. Wearing a girdle (like the old-fashioned corsets) can help improve back support and lessen slumping over time.
Aim for 10,000 steps a day to improve your overall health and well-being.

Maintaining Weight Loss

Maintaining weight loss is difficult. How can you do it? Extreme rapid weight loss hypnosis for women! The program will help you to become aware of what you are eating and when; reduce your appetite by aiding your body in releasing less insulin and raising leptin (the hormone responsible for making you feel full); cut cravings by teaching your body to process different types of foods more efficiently; help avoid binge eating by breaking bad habits and therefore prolonging the time between binges, as well as reducing the severity of those binges.
Actions of Extreme Rapid Weight Loss Hypnosis for Women:

The main benefit of this program is the ability to program your weight loss. Our Rapid Weight Loss Hypnosis for women audio program will help you lose weight rapidly and naturally by breaking bad habits and foods that cause cravings. You can now restart your diet at a new level. The results are dramatic. No more body fat in 6 months or even one year! This hypnosis is easy to follow, so you can do it from the privacy of home or office and keep losing weight effectively.

The program is a combination of hypnosis, neuro-linguistic programming, and NLP technology. The creator of this technique is Dr. Ivan Pavlov, a Russian physiologist who won the Nobel Prize in medicine. This behavior modification system can influence areas of the mind that you do not even know to exist. It reinforces your motivation to permanently lose weight by making you believe that to be healthy; one must maintain a proper weight.

How Does Rapid Weight Loss Hypnosis Work?

What is Rapid Weight Loss Hypnosis? You may be surprised to find out that hypnosis won't make you lose weight overnight or turn fat into muscles, as many people believe it does. However, it does provide you with the tools to lose weight more efficiently and effectively.

In hypnosis, your mind is guided into a state where it can achieve a deep level of relaxation and concentration. This allows you to take charge of your thoughts and feelings by changing what goes through your mind and overriding the negative thoughts that make you want to eat unhealthy food for no reason. In this way, you learn how to listen to your body's signals or instincts; recognize when you are hungry; choose healthier foods when eating out or at home; stop eating when full; and much more.

More and more women follow the "yo-yo dieting" pattern, although they do not want to do so. This pattern of behavior is caused by the loss of motivation that usually comes with weight loss. This affects all people who want to lose weight and keep it off for good. The best way to lose weight and keep it off is through hypnosis.
Weight loss has many other benefits from overcoming an emotional problem rather than an actual physical one. Once you have made up your mind to follow strict diet plans, you will also feel more confident about yourself and less likely to overeat.

It will be easier to say "No" to unhealthy snacks when you feel good about yourself and your willpower. This is why hypnosis can give you the motivation necessary for long-lasting weight loss.

It takes ten pounds of pressure against a balloon to burst, but once that pressure is released, the balloon can become re-inflated with ease.

The course is designed for all women, not just those who have a weight problem. It teaches self-confidence, self-awareness, and practical thinking skills that are transferable to any area of life.

In the course, you will be guided through several sessions and slowly introduced to techniques to increase your self-esteem. These include visualization techniques, which will help you keep at it and resist giving up when you feel weak or exhausted.

Take-home sessions are available to help women learn how to incorporate these new skills into everyday situations. This enables them to avoid emotional triggers that might aggravate their weight issue and make more independent decisions about what they eat and how they respond to the food environment around them.
Almost everyone knows getting weight loss supplements does not always work.

You will be able to:

- Work on your weight loss plan and keep track of your progress.

- Learn to make intuitive decisions that are beneficial to you and apply them wherever possible.

- Set reasonable goals for yourself, then gradually work towards them.

This will help you to avoid setting unrealistic targets.

- Create your own fast weight loss hypnosis session; this will help you to focus on the task at hand.

- Learn how to lose weight rapidly using a smooth, steady diet over a shorter period.

-Take control of your eating habits and manage cravings, make decisions for yourself, and feel in control.

- Understand why some people can eat less than their peers despite coping with stresses in their lives, while others struggle against their cravings for food even though they have everything going for them.

- Empower yourself by permitting yourself to make choices that fit your lifestyle while understanding positive changes will benefit you as well as others.

- Learn how to deal with binge eating and other weight loss problems.
I am looking forward to seeing you on the program!

The 17 Best Ways to Maintain Weight Loss

Shockingly, numerous individuals who get thinner wind up restoring it.
Just about 20% of calorie counters who get going overweight end up effectively getting thinner and keeping it off in the long haul.

Notwithstanding, don't allow this to debilitate you. There are various experimentally demonstrated ways to keep the load off, going from practicing to controlling pressure.
These 17 systems may be exactly what you need to tip the insights in support of yourself and keep up your hard-won weight reduction

1. Exercise Often
Exercising for in any event 30 minutes of the day may advance weight upkeep by aiding balance your calories in and calories consumed

2. Take a stab at Eating Breakfast Every Day
The individuals who have breakfast will have better propensities by and large, which may assist them with keeping up their weight. In any case, skipping breakfast doesn't naturally prompt weight acquire.
3. Eat Lots of Protein

Protein may profit weight upkeep by advancing completion, expanding digestion, and diminishing your total calorie admission.
4. Weigh Yourself Regularly

Self-weighing may help weight upkeep by keeping you mindful of your advancement and practices.
5. Be Mindful of Your Carb Intake

Restricting your admission of carbs, particularly those that are refined, may help forestall weight recapture
6. Lift Weights

Lifting loads in any event double seven days may assist with weight support by saving your bulk, which is critical to support solid digestion.
7. Be Prepared for Setbacks

Almost certainly, you will experience a mishap or two in the wake of getting thinner. You can defeat mishaps by preparing and refocusing immediately.

8. Stick to Your Plan All Week Long (Even on Weekends)
Effective weight upkeep is simpler to achieve when you adhere to your good dieting propensities the entire week, remembering for ends of the week

9. Stay Hydrated
Drinking water regularly may advance completion and increment your digestion, both significant components in weight upkeep.

10. Get Enough Sleep
Resting for solid periods may assist with weight support by keeping your energy step up and chemicals leveled out.

11. Control Stress Levels
It is essential to monitor feelings of anxiety to keep up your weight, as abundance stress may expand the danger of weight acquire by invigorating your hunger.

12. Find a Support System
Including an accomplice or life partner in your reliable way of life may help the probability that you will keep up your weight reduction.

13. Track Your Food Intake
Logging your food admission from one day to another may assist you with keeping up your weight reduction by making you mindful of the number of calories and supplements you're eating.

14. Eat Plenty of Vegetables
Vegetables are high in fiber and low in calories. Both of these properties might be useful for weight support.

15. Be Consistent
Keeping up weight reduction is essential when you are predictable with your new solid propensities instead of returning to your old way of life.

16. Practice Mindful Eating

Careful eating is helpful for weight support since it assists you with perceiving completion and may forestall undesirable practices that regularly lead to weight acquire.

17. Make Sustainable Changes to Your Lifestyle

It is simpler to keep up weight reduction when you make the reasonable way of life changes, instead of observing the ridiculous standards that many weight reduction consumes fewer calories center around.

The Bottom Line

Diets can be prohibitive and unreasonable, which frequently prompts weight recapture.
In any case, you can make a lot of fundamental changes to your propensities that are not difficult to stay with and will assist you with keeping up your weight reduction in the long haul.

Through your excursion, you will understand that controlling your weight includes significantly more than what you eat. Exercise, rest, and psychological well-being additionally assume apart.

It is workable for weight support to be easy on the off chance that you essentially embrace another way of life instead of going on and off weight reduction eats less.

"The New York Times" chose "The China Study: The Most Comprehensive Study of Nutrition Ever Conducted And the Startling Implications for Diet, Weight Loss, and Long-term Health" as one of its "Best Books of the Year 2009".
The book is also featured on the cover of "Time Magazine," "Scientific American," and other journals and magazines.

In 2014, Dr. Campbell announced a new project that would update his 1999 study by assessing the health outcomes from dietary interventions worldwide with data from over 200 countries. This project is known as The China Study 2.0, or "CST 2." The study will be released in 2016.

How to Use Affirmation for Weight Loss

Weight loss affirmations for women are a popular and effective way to help your mind work with you in your weight loss goals. When combined with hypnosis, studies have found that they can yield significant benefits for those who want to lose weight. Usually, the best approach is to combine hypnosis and affirmations with other ways of losing weight, such as dieting, exercise, or self-hypnosis. In this post, we look at how affirmation can be used for weight loss and give you a list of our top choices for alternative methods too!

Combining hypnotherapy and affirmations into a healthy lifestyle is more beneficial than using either option on its own. This is because the different approaches have certain advantages over the other, and they can complement each other to produce even better effects. If you use them both, you will be able to combine the benefits of each option which could include losing weight, gaining confidence, improving motivation levels, and more. Below we look at both hypnotherapy for weight loss and affirmations for weight loss. We also provide a list of our favorite claims for weight loss too!

How can hypnotherapy help me lose weight?

Hypnosis works with your mind by combining suggestions with relaxation techniques to get you more motivated towards your goal and make it easier for you to achieve this goal. The most effective way to use hypnosis for weight loss is to combine it with some type of diet or exercise plan. This way, you will not have any problems motivating yourself to stick to your goals, and you can do this by using an effective weight loss hypnosis. Another great benefit of using hypnosis for weight loss is that it has shown to be more effective than other ways of losing weight, such as diets and exercising.

Why should I use affirmations for weight loss?

Affirmations are used in the same way as hypnotherapy to help you change your mindset and attitude. The most critical part of using assertions for weight loss is how you react to them. If you have negative thoughts about yourself or feel that you are not good enough, then these will pass and become something true for you. However, about 75% of people who use affirmations do not get the results they expect from them, which is why the following list looks at the more effective claims for weight loss that works best!

Most effective affirmations to lose weight – TOP 12

These are our top ten favorite affirmations for weight loss which have been proven to work best. The ones listed here have helped our free online hypnosis community members and often produce great short-term results.

1. I am a healthy person

People find this affirmation very effective because it starts by saying "I." This is an excellent way to start as it implies that you are in control and have accepted yourself for who you are. This is listed as one of the top 10 affirmations for weight loss because it helps to build positive emotions towards yourself and your body. This allows you to accept your body type and makes your weight loss goals easier to achieve. It also encourages positive thinking, which helps make both short-term and long-term goals much easier to achieve.

2. I can control my eating

People who have difficulty controlling their eating often find that this affirmation helps them start trusting their bodies. By starting with a simple commitment such as "I can control my eating," you are showing yourself that you are in control and trust yourself more. This will make it easier for you to regain control of your eating habits and help you lose weight. The second part of this affirmation is essential because it allows people who have problems controlling their eating. After all, they often think that they cannot do anything about it. You need to focus on the second part of this affirmation because if you focus on the first part, this will stop working for you.

3. I choose only healthy foods for me

This is another good affirmation for people who are having problems with controlling their eating. It helps to show them that they have power over what they eat and choose to eat only healthy foods. By affirming this, you are reinforcing the idea of eating only healthy foods, which helps you break any bad habits that you have formed and it also helps you start developing habits that will help you lose weight. You should repeat this affirmation as much as possible whenever you feel like eating something unhealthy. Say it out loud if possible or in your head if this is easier for you.

4. I will be motivated to lose weight

This affirmation is very similar to saying, "I am motivated." It helps you reflect on how you are feeling about losing weight, and it also allows you to feel motivated. This makes it easier for you to continue your hypnotherapy sessions, but it can also help you stop thinking about losing weight and focusing on other things. If this is going through your mind a lot, then use this affirmation as an alternative to concentrating on losing weight because it is much easier.

5. I will eat small amounts of food at a time

This affirmation can be used when eating food to help you stop binge eating and stop overeating. By telling yourself that you will only eat small amounts of food, you reinforce good habits, which enables you to break bad habits. It would help if you did not repeat this affirmation too often because it can become a bad habit. It would help if you said it once or twice before you start eating something and then use your willpower to stop yourself from overeating.

6. I will be very proud of myself

This is an excellent affirmation for those who feel down about themselves and don't feel as if they are good enough to lose weight. You should say this affirmation out loud, and you should say it as often as possible while focusing on your weight loss goals. You will feel very proud of yourself when you see that you have shed much weight in a short space of time.

7. I have my whole life to lose weight

This affirmation is very effective for those struggling to achieve their weight loss goals because they often get caught up in thinking about the future and how long everything will take. This affirmation helps them think positively and helps them focus on the present instead of thinking about what can go wrong with their diet or how long it is going to take for them to lose weight. This affirmation helps to motivate them to lose weight, and it also helps them not give up too quickly.

8. I am learning new things every day

This affirmation is excellent for helping you look at losing weight differently. It is used before starting a weight loss program, and it allows you to realize that there is always something new for you to learn about losing weight because there are many different ways you can do this. This affirmation also helps you to feel motivated and excited about losing weight instead of feeling downhearted by yourself or those around you who are not doing as well as you.

9. I am a hot goddess, and I deserve to be healthy

This affirmation is excellent for helping you feel confident about the way you look at yourself. It makes you feel good about yourself and the way that you look at yourself. It would be best if you said this affirmation aloud as often as possible to make it a part of your life. Remember to repeat it whenever and wherever possible because it is essential to use this affirmation as often as likely to be successful.

10. I have all the time in the world to lose weight

This affirmation helps those struggling with their weight loss goals because they often forget how long they have to achieve their goals. This is why this affirmation is great because it reminds those who have a problem with weight loss that they are not in a hurry to lose weight. They can do this, and they should do it because they have all the time in the world.

11. I am on my way to becoming thinner

This affirmation is excellent for those of you who may be looking at losing weight differently. It will give you some motivation to lose weight and change your life for the better. This affirmation works well if you want something different than the typical weight loss affirmations out there.

12. I love myself, and I am proud to stand in my light

This affirmation is great for anyone who is trying to lose weight. If you can learn to love yourself after losing a few pounds, then you are more likely to stay with it. The real key is to accept that you have in your hands the power to make a difference, even if it means making small changes over time.

Beneficial Affirmation to Use for Weight Loss

Beneficial affirmation to use for weight loss: "I am strong and healthy, I am slim and trim."

Every woman wants to be slim and trim. This is especially true when it comes to the summer months when all of your friends show off their bodies. But how do you achieve that? Is there a quick fix? Fortunately, there is a way of achieving weight loss through hypnosis. The secret lies in extreme rapid weight loss hypnosis for women, which guarantees dramatic results in as little as three days.

That's why we've put together this post all about how to go about extreme rapid weight loss hypnosis for women — complete with what it is, what it does, and presumably speaks for itself.

What is extreme rapid weight loss hypnosis?

Extreme rapid weight loss hypnosis is a reliable and effective way of achieving your ideal body shape. The majority of us desire a lean and firm stomach, but the question is, how do we achieve it? Well, this hypnosis program is specifically designed to help you attain your dreams. The fast weight-loss method can be practiced at home in the comfort of your surroundings — all you need are your headphones.

Does extreme rapid weight loss hypnosis work?

Yes! We have had hundreds of lives transformed thanks to extreme rapid weight loss hypnosis. Thousands of people worldwide are now in control and have lost countless pounds with this incredible program.

What are the benefits of extreme rapid weight loss hypnosis?

The benefits of extreme rapid weight loss hypnosis are immeasurable. You will be able to reduce your body weight by up to ten pounds in no time! The program is designed to help you lose weight fast while also improving your appearance and making you healthier. The fast weight loss method is also safe, natural, and recommended by medical professionals. Thousands of people around the world have used this program successfully.

When does extreme rapid weight loss hypnosis work?

Extreme rapid weight loss hypnosis is designed specifically for women and works best during the summer months. You will lose as much as three pounds per week, which is very reasonable.

How long will it take to lose ten pounds through extreme rapid weight loss hypnosis?

It would help if you aimed for a result within three weeks of use. You may be able to achieve your goal within 48 hours. If you're not impressed, check out the testimonials or ask a friend to try it out for you! Everybody's different, but our clients all claim that they lost around 3 pounds per day.

How much weight will you lose?

You will lose between 3 and 10 pounds in three days, which is very impressive. Our clients, on average, lose 4 pounds per day. There is no need to worry, though, as the weight loss doesn't stop at ten pounds. You can keep going until you reach your goal weight.

What does extreme rapid weight loss hypnosis feel like?

Because extreme rapid weight loss hypnosis is not a medical procedure, there are no side effects. However, you will be hypnotized, which is not mandatory. You can opt for the release option if you wish. The hypnosis experience is completely safe! However, it won't feel like anything other than a normal state of deep relaxation; you will not be in any pain or discomfort.

Of course! You can listen to extreme rapid weight loss hypnosis on your own or with a group of friends and family members. This program was designed with the utmost care to ensure that everybody enjoys it safely and without any problems. We also offer a free consultation to discuss your entire experience and ask any questions that may arise during your experience using this program.

How to use extreme rapid weight loss hypnosis?

The first step is to find a comfortable spot to sit. You can listen with your eyes closed or with your headphones on, but this is not mandatory. You can even take the mp3 player into the bathroom if you like! Next, relax for a few minutes while listening to the unique audio tracks. Lastly, re-focus on your intentions and go about your day as you usually would. Within a few days, you will start noticing positive differences in your body!

Which program should I try?

Both extreme rapid weight loss hypnotherapy programs are pretty similar; however, one is aimed towards women, intended for men. They both work in the same way but with a slightly different focus. So if you are looking to lose weight quickly and safely, try our extreme rapid weight loss hypnosis program for women!

I can listen to extreme rapid weight loss hypnosis on my own or with a group of friends and family members. This program was designed with the utmost care to ensure that everybody enjoys it safely and without any problems. We also offer a free consultation to discuss your entire experience and ask any questions that may arise during your experience using this program.

How quickly will I lose weight?

The great thing about extreme rapid weight loss hypnosis is that you can lose as much weight as you want, but the process is safe and natural. That means you don't have to worry at all about your health or safety! However, in terms of how long it takes to experience results, some users lose as much as 10 lbs. in a week! But you don't have to wait to see how well this works; try it for yourself right away!

Is extreme rapid weight loss hypnosis effective?

Yes! Extreme rapid weight loss hypnosis is based on many years of clinical research. Currently, there are millions of people around the world who have experienced radical, rapid weight loss hypnosis during their private sessions, as well as hundreds of thousands who have had the opportunity to find out firsthand how effective it is! That means that this program works for most people.

Train Your Brain to Love Exercise

Train your brain to love exercise and to eat healthily.

Hypnosis is one of the easiest ways to change your habits. The mind controls our actions and behaviors to change how we act by changing what we think about. Hypnosis can be used when you have an important event coming up (like a wedding or a reunion) or changing habits like going to sleep earlier or exercising more.

Hypnotherapy for weight loss has been shown to help people have healthier food choices and improve the quality of their workouts without depending on expensive supplements and programs that are too hard to maintain long term. Hypnosis for weight loss has also been shown to be a reasonably effective treatment for binge eating disorder, which is a severe issue. If you are looking to lose weight and have the willpower to make it happen, hypnotherapy is a great way to do it.

If you struggle with being able to stick with an exercise plan long-term or want someone else coaching you during your workouts (and aren't shy about asking them for help), hypnosis can be helpful. There are special programs available specifically for people who have issues sticking with their exercise programs and teaching you how to make the most of your workout time.

Globally, people are increasingly turning to hypnosis for weight loss. While the general population is on the rise, many other factors could explain this trend. We have seen a steady increase in hypnotic practices and results over the last ten years in the US. Many people opt for hypnotherapy due to its products, such as better success rates of weight loss and creating lasting changes in eating habits and exercise routines.

Hypnosis provides various benefits that cannot be found in most psychotherapy techniques or through diet and exercise alone. This is because hypnosis has been proven to work with the subconscious mind. The subconscious mind is one of the most potent areas of your brain and cannot be ignored or commanded by anyone else. This means that hypnosis works best when you can get to know what it wants and then reach into that part of your mind with positive suggestions, along with positive visualization techniques, to make changes in habits or behaviors.

To get the most out of any program designed for weight loss, you have to make sure that you are giving it your full attention. If you are doing things on the side or distracting yourself with new things, you may not get the full benefit from this program. Hypnosis is an excellent tool for stress relief that will help you get into a routine and focus on what you are trying to accomplish. By getting rid of some of the stress in your life, you will be better able to focus on making changes in your habits and behaviors.

As with any weight loss program, hypnotherapy is designed to help people make long-term changes in their diet and exercise routine so that they can lose weight and keep it off. Even if you only lose a few pounds, hypnosis can help you keep it off for more extended periods. While counting calories and changing your eating habits is one of the most important things to do during a hypnotherapy program, other techniques can be beneficial.

To get started on any weight loss program, you need to make sure that you have some goals in mind. A great way to have these goals and keep them in front of your mind is through positive visualization techniques. These tools are straightforward and can be done quickly with some practice.

When you are trying to lose weight, you need to make sure that you have a good plan. You can do this by creating a program with a series of steps to help you get where you want to be. The best way to make positive changes in your life is by having some motivation and routine. Hypnosis can be a very effective way to form habits and change your life.

To lose weight through hypnosis, you have to make sure that you have a plan for what you will do. Many people make the mistake of trying hypnosis once and then think they are done with it when they don't see immediate results. While some people see results right away, most people need several sessions before they begin to notice effects. Like any program or change in life, there will be some effort required on your part, but the results will be worth it in the end.

It is essential to set a goal weight that you are looking to achieve. If you are unsure where to start, it is best to choose a target weight that will not be too far off from your current weight. This will help you stick with the program and reach your goal more quickly. Once you have this number in mind, it is essential to keep track of your progress to measure and see how much progress you have made. The catch is that if your efforts don't match what your brain wants, it will not stop at this point. The person's brain will create another plan based on its information, leading to a vicious cycle. Therefore, if you want to stop this cycle and lose weight, you need to create a new plan.

Hypnosis is a powerful tool used in many different areas of a person's life. Weight loss hypnosis has become especially popular in recent years. This is because it is effective with long-term results that are hard to get through other programs or exercises alone. Many people have found that they can finally get where they want to be with their weight loss goals by combining hypnosis and training.

There is a lot of hype out there when it comes to hypnosis and weight loss. Many people think that by simply listening to a tape, they will lose weight overnight. The truth is that like any other type of exercise or diet plan out there, hypnosis will take some work on your part. It is important to remember that if you are serious about losing weight, you need to commit and follow through with it until it has been achieved. Hypnosis may be a powerful tool, but it is only as effective as what you put into it.

If you are thinking about trying hypnosis for weight loss, you may find yourself struggling with whether or not you want to accomplish this goal in the first place. So many people doubt whether or not they are ready for hypnosis to help them lose weight because they have tried many other methods without success. Many people find themselves vicious cycle of trying one new way after another for weight loss with no actual results.

While it is true that hypnosis can work very well in the area of weight loss, you need to make sure that you are ready for it. This can be very difficult because most of us struggle to lose a few pounds but feel like we cannot do it because we have already tried everything else. It is important to remember that you are not a failure and need to give hypnosis a fair chance. If you find that it does not work for you, it is simply because it was not the right fit for your brain. You will then be free to try something new with no guilt or self-doubt getting in the way of your success.

Another common misconception about hypnosis for weight loss is that you can listen to the tape or use the program as many times as needed until you have achieved your goal. While this may seem very logical, it will lead to some serious problems later on. If you have listened to the tape or used the program so many times that you have not lost any weight, then your brain will begin to associate hearing to those tapes or attending the sessions with weight loss as a whole. This will, in turn, cause your brain to continue to think that listening is necessary to help you lose weight.

If you want to achieve lasting weight loss through hypnosis, there are a few things that you need to think about and decide for it to be effective. One thing is that you need to know if hypnosis is right for you. If you believe that it is not, then it is just best to try other alternatives.

If you have tried most weight loss methods and have not been able to lose weight, you may want to try hypnosis at least. You need to make sure that you are entirely open-minded when giving this a shot because this can easily influence your brain. You need to make sure that you think deeply about why you do not want to try hypnosis before making any decisions on this matter. If, for whatever reason, hypnosis does not seem like the right option, then go ahead and take a look at some of the other diet programs or weight loss methods out there.

Effortlessly Burn Fat

Effortlessly burn fat without dieting.

End cravings in just days.

Feel energetic, confident, and sexy at any weight for life. What if you could have a body that looked as good as it feels? Your body is the vehicle for your life - so why not treat it like a Ferrari? With hypnosis to melt fat fast and turn every bite into power, you can eat whatever you want, whenever you want, without ever getting fat again! We'll guide you through processes to effortlessly burn away all the layers of stubborn extra fat on your belly or thighs and find your physique sexy again. With daily hypnosis sessions, you will effortlessly let go of all your negative feelings toward yourself that made you eat in the first place.

This is real hypnotic work - not quick fixes, but long-lasting changes to your lifestyle and eating habits that become second nature.
Join us now on this exciting journey to discover more of the real you and take control of your life!

The Diet Trap: How a Crash Diet or Binge Can Make You Fatter

When you diet, your body goes into starvation mode. It slows down the metabolism to conserve energy to survive without food for as long as possible.

Weight loss - yes, it's possible. But it's not easy, and nothing is more discouraging than watching weight creep back on after years of success.

"The Diet Trap" describes three common diet traps:

How to beat the diet trap: 3 common diet traps and how to avoid them.

Hypnosis for Weight Loss & Emotional Eating Free MP3 Download!

(And a free download of our hypnosis cd "Weight Loss From The Inside Out" to find out what makes you eat.)

Let me share with you my own story...

I remember the first time I saw a picture of myself in the mirror. It was a time when I knew that I had to make a change in my life, and of course, there was nothing more motivating than looking better physically. When I heard about hypnosis, I thought it sounded like just what I needed to get rid of excess fat and make other changes in my life.

But even though the other changes were essential to me, losing weight was the only thing that mattered at that moment. So when someone suggested hypnosis as a way to get rid of some extra fat, it wasn't difficult for me to sign up.

I was a member of a weight loss hypnosis group for three weeks ... and I ended up gaining back all the weight I had lost.
And that's when I got the idea to hypnotize myself. Of course, it made perfect sense to me at the time, but now I see it as very silly and even dangerous.

That's because, to be successful with hypnosis, you need to believe that your subconscious is working for you instead of against you. And I don't think that's possible when you've been unsuccessful in the past with dieting.

Hypnosis isn't something that you can do on the spur of the moment. You need a commitment to pursue it as a lifestyle, something you'll continue even after trying hypnosis for weight loss and finding it doesn't work for you. Hypnosis is about being willing to make changes in your life, not about just thinking about them.

I had a severe lack of self-confidence... but that's never been a problem for me. My values include being honest, good with people, and always doing the right thing. Even though I didn't want to admit it to myself, I knew that I was worth more than what I was doing to myself.

I met my husband on the Internet, and at first, we only talked a few times... until he called and asked me out on our first actual date ever! When he told me his life story, I realized that he was very similar to me in many ways...

And when we were finally married... things started to change for us....
Suddenly we were sharing everything; our feelings, our goals, and so on. And then one day, I thought about something that I hadn't realized before...

Hypnosis to Lose Weight: The Pros and Cons of Using Hypnosis

The Pros:

Burn more calories when you sleep - up to 300 a night!
Melt belly fat and other stubborn fat areas more accessible than ever before!
Lose weight faster without starving or dieting at all.

The Cons:

You can screw up your metabolism by drastically changing your diet or exercising too much. That's why we recommend taking things slowly and making changes gradually.

It would help if you practiced hypnosis regularly. That means you'll need to do at least one session per week. Or you might only be able to do one session per month.
Instead of eating less, it's more likely that you'll end up eating more and feeling stuffed - which can lead to cravings for more and making it harder to lose weight or stop overeating.

Your attitude toward food can still be harmful even after the weight loss has stopped unless you regularly practice hypnosis.

You might be able to develop a fear of overeating... which is a genuine possibility.

When you drop down to your ideal weight, something that hypnosis can help you with, you might become paranoid about food and gaining the weight back.

But indeed, these reasons aren't enough for you to avoid trying hypnosis for weight loss? If it's something that could work for you... shouldn't you give it a chance?

I'm going to get into a lot more detail about how hypnosis works in just a few minutes... but first, I want to talk about my own experience with it.

I knew that hypnosis was probably too good to be true, though. I figured that if it worked... my stomach muscles might be able to tighten up so much with just a few sessions of hypnosis.

I wanted to know for myself whether or not we could lose weight simply by doing some imagination exercises... and then let our subconscious do all the rest. I finally decided to work with a hypnotherapist when we moved into his home office so he could administer the hypnosis in person instead of having me do it while on the phone.

One session went very well... but I also imagined many things that didn't pan out. I believed that if I succeeded in "imagining" myself thin... then my actual body would change to match that imaginary body. The funny thing is, even though we never changed our diet... I still thought we were losing weight!

I thought hypnosis had worked... and then it looked like it hadn't worked. At the end of the first hypnosis session, the hypnotist asked if I wanted to get up, walk around the room with him, leave the office, and come back once he hypnotized me again.

I didn't feel like walking around in a big circle anymore, so I agreed to do it again some other time. After we got home, I started thinking... maybe I didn't do things as well the second time around because of moving the chair around in place.

If the chair was sitting in a different spot, why wasn't it working this time?

It didn't make any sense... but it wouldn't go away. And the more that idea plagued me, the more confused I became. I tried to remember how every single thing about our hypnosis session went so well... and yet nothing seemed to be working!

I started to feel personally responsible for what was going on with my body. If I had done it right, if I had followed the rules exactly, then what was going on? All of a sudden, that first hypnotist's voice seemed to come alive in my head... and he was telling me that he was disappointed in me.

I thought, no... this isn't happening. I started to cry as I imagined him telling me how I wasn't living up to my potential and how there was nothing wrong with my body except that "I" wasn't doing other things with it - like exercise.

He gave me advice about the way to harness the power of hypnosis and get rid of bad habits... and he was also telling me that I was a "bad girl" and that my body was suffering because of it.

This wasn't happening - I was just in a hypnotic trance! At that point, I started to panic. Did I do something wrong? Had I been doing all that stuff the wrong way? Shouldn't my subconscious be able to take care of this?!

I started getting very anxious... very quickly.

And this anxiety grew worse day after day.

What if I have ruined my subconscious? How can I get it back to the state where it knows what I want and makes my life go like a movie? What if I can't do it?! And even more horrifying... What if it never gets better?!

THE SLOW, LONG WAY...

It was then that I discovered hypnosis. And how hypnosis can be used to help me with this problem. I said to myself that since hypnosis seemed like a good solution, then there must be an easy way I could use to hypnotize myself whenever I wanted.

It seemed apparent that I could put myself under and do things to myself that might help me without doing it in a way that was so complicated. It seemed like it would be even easier for me to accomplish with hypnosis than any other method I had tried.

But the idea of my subconscious being affected by what I did or didn't do... and then not having anything happen... scared the hell out of me. That kind of thing could happen with hypnosis. After all, there was still no guarantee that it would work for me.

I don't know how to say this without sounding like a total wimp... but I was terrified of using hypnosis for weight loss. I knew it would take much time and work... and I didn't want to try. I needed something else as an incentive or needed to find a different way to make the program easier for me.
That is when I discovered negative thoughts, which are an obstacle for many people trying hypnosis for weight loss. If you can clear those doubts out of your mind, then you'll be able to succeed faster with hypnosis and get on the fast track to weight loss.

Even though it had worked for me with other things, we tried... I couldn't help but wonder if this was working this time. Even after I had finally gotten over my fear of using hypnosis... I came to a realization that made me almost glad it hadn't worked for me.

I thought about all the things we were going to do in our sessions... but even though some of them sounded nice and fun, the feeling that your body could change so dramatically overnight was enough to make me want to stop right then and there.
All this talk about changing your body sounds like it would be incredible... but let's face it... someday, we'll wake up and find out that it didn't happen at all.

Increase Motivation

Increase motivation and achieve your weight loss goals fast with hypnosis. Hypnotherapy for weight loss is a popular and effective way of overcoming overeating and emotional eating, dieting, fasting, and compulsive eating.
Hypnosis has been used for decades by doctors and medical professionals to help people lose excess weight. Hypnosis for weight loss is a powerful, natural, non-surgical way to help you shed those extra pounds. The words "weight loss" can have a negative connotation. However, nothing is more important than your health.

What Is Hypnosis for Weight Loss?

Hypnotism is a very natural way to help you lose weight. The key to weight loss hypnosis is the subconscious mind – that part of your brain where habits and behavior are put into action. Dr. Verne Golden explains this in his book, "Blunder Woman: The Hypnotic Adventures of a Weight Loss Doctor." The book describes how hypnosis can induce positive changes in people's behaviors (like eating healthier foods) and attitudes about food and exercise.

Hypnosis for Weight Loss Also Uses the Subconscious Mind

The subconscious mind consists of a multitude of our thoughts, behaviors, and feelings. This is sometimes called the "unconscious" because we don't have control over it. However, we do have control over the thoughts and behaviors put into action by the conscious mind. We can choose what we think and feel every day by using techniques like meditation and hypnosis.

In this hypnosis recording for weight loss, you will effortlessly:

* Reduce your desire to overeat and eat compulsively

* Gain better self-confidence and self-esteem as you begin to shed the excess weight off of your body

* Feel motivated and inspired towards continuing your journey of success toward achieving your ideal weight.

This hypnosis recording is designed to listen to a minimum of 3 times per week with a one-month commitment. You will begin to notice changes in your eating habits, self-confidence, and ability to eat less than you want after listening to the hypnosis audio recording just once.

Hypnotherapy for women often focuses on food rituals, trigger foods, body image issues, fears about being overweight or underweight. Our Los Angeles hypnotherapist at Hypnotiques has helped people with weight-related problems lose anywhere from 10 pounds to 200 pounds!

Our Los Angeles hypnotherapist is Dr. Scott Langley, who has been in private practice since 1995. He is a certified hypnotherapist, life coach, and weight loss specialist. Dr. Langley has successfully worked with hundreds of people who are struggling with their weight.

Motivations

Motivation is the power of your appetite and everything you would like.
Needing is a sense which you're able to control. For the majority of your life, you've primarily controlled your appetite or desire by restricting or denying it. You could be rather good at managing your wants and needs in specific regions and weak or unpractised in others. Since this is a "diet" book, you might have already prepared to listen to this "diet," which would probably be similar to others who have informed you what you have to deny to limit yourself.

In other words, other diets also have told you precisely what not to desire, and the accent might have been about "not needing" a few foods you have grown to appreciate. Welcome to a different method of treating yourself. We will invite you to get better at "wanting." Denial isn't contained in The Self-Hypnosis Diet.

Your motivation is a crucial variable among the fundamental and fundamental ingredients. We would like you to concentrate your energy on needing motivation, which informs your mind-body of everything you would like to get to ideal weight. We invite you to get great at wanting your perfect weight. Here's a good illustration. Let's suppose that you're in a pool, and you breathe in a mouthful of water. In that instant, you need just 1 item, a breath of air. It seems like death or life and a breath of all.

The atmosphere is the one thing on your head currently. The needing is so powerful and intense that it overshadows the rest of the ideas. And propels one to do anything which is required to find that breath of air. That's just how much we would like you to need the exact burden and body image you want. We desire you to hold the need so firm that it overshadows everything. Here's a good illustration. Once you've been crushed to death, your brain will be highly vulnerable to seeing your thoughts and feeling such a need that getting back out of the debris is simply overpowering.

Your mind will not be able to say no to it because it means survival and vitality. And all the desires are what sustain survival and life. The best word to describe the craving is "wanting." It's good, not like "needing" as an energy source.

BELIEF AND THINKING

Beliefs are such ideas that are accurate for you. They don't need to be proven that you understand them to be authentic for you. Whether you're conscious of it or not, your activities, unconscious and conscious, are according to your own beliefs. Though your beliefs come in the shape of ideas and thoughts, they form your expertise by changing your activities in life. If you feel that animals make fantastic companions, then you most likely have a dog or cat or parrot or a ferret or two. If you think that coffee keeps you awake during the night, you most likely don't drink coffee before bed.

The energy of thinking permits you to affect your entire body in a way that may appear astonishing.

Placebo answers, where folks respond to an inert chemical as though it were the correct medicine, are typical examples of how beliefs have been experienced within the entire body. If an individual believes he will become well when carrying a specific treatment, it will take place if the pill includes drugs or is only perceptible. In precisely the same manner, if an individual believes he can attain high school levels, it will occur. If an individual thinks he can reach his ideal weight, then it is going to happen.

Recall your chosen matches as a kid. Your capacity to feign is equally as powerful now as if you're young. It might be a little rusty, and you may require a bit of exercise, but when you allow yourself to feign and think what you're pretending, you will see a powerful instrument.

You will find that this can be a superbly productive method to achieve your aims, these messages of everything you would like, to everyone, the cells, organs, and tissues of the human body, which reacts by bringing that aim to reality for you. We cannot state these ideas or things. The views, the images, and thoughts you set in your head become the messages that your self-hypnosis communicates into a mind-body, finally turning your ideal body into a truth. Pretending is picking what to think and getting absorbed in these thoughts. As a magnifying glass may concentrate beams of the sun, you can focus your emotional energy to create your ideas, reviews, and beliefs for your physique.

The Self-Hypnosis Diet is not as mysterious as you may think. It is an efficient and functional alternative approach to losing weight. You can be aware that if you're not familiar with this form of dieting, it may appear somewhat weird. Also, recall that the important thing factor is that your body responds very well to the message that you send every day. This is especially so when you use self-hypnosis for the language. With The Self-Hypnosis Diet, many people have succeeded in shedding their weight in an easier way than they anticipated.

You can make use of self-hypnosis for this diet, also if you've never tried it before. You'll be able to make use of self-hypnosis tools to inform your body that you are going to eat a high-quality diet and that you will not allow it to be fat. You'll then be able to use your self-hypnosis technique for the Self-Hypnosis Diet and see many results.

A fundamental principle in the Self-Hypnosis Diet is achieving a nutritious plan which supports this weight loss. When it comes time for you to select your meals, you have to remember that fat is bad. Do not eat anything found in the foods section, on the shelves, produced by any means other than plant material or animal components.

Many people have difficulty following a healthy diet since they get too hungry or feel that they cannot handle the strain. You'll find that if you follow the Self-Hypnosis Diet, you will not get hungry. You may also be pleasantly surprised to find that the weight starts melting off around your waistline and other parts of your body. The calories you're eating will be stored in a different part of the body than fat so that you will see a reduction in fat at first. After some time on the diet, you'll start to lose inches from your waistline.

The Self-Hypnosis Diet is an excellent option for those who want to shed weight effectively. This works because you do not struggle to keep the weight off, as because of the suggestion you get from self-hypnosis, you will carry it off and maintain it off. This diet may be followed by anyone with a desire to lose weight.

Self-Hypnosis Diet can be used by anybody who needs to shed weight. You might have tried other methods of losing weight, but you realize that they are not effective. It's possible that you haven't tried any other diet, but if it doesn't work for your body type or circumstances, then they won't be effective either. The Self-Hypnosis Diet was created for people who feel discouraged about their ability and their situation when shedding fat.

If you're ready to adopt self-hypnosis to reduce weight, you need to follow the directions in this book. It will take you step by step through the diet and self-hypnosis sessions necessary to lose weight.

The Self-Hypnosis Diet is a diet plan that includes self-hypnosis for inducing rapid weight loss. The diet plan is based on a healthy eating plan, food supplements, and eating habits that doctors and nutritionists have recommended. The Self-Hypnosis Diet book presents an approach to weight loss that combines nutritional principles with hypnotherapy for rapid results. It combines hypnotherapy with information on nutrition and healthy eating habits presented in easy-to-understand language.

The Self-Hypnosis Diet book is intended for those who are tired of using diets that don't work and those who want to lose weight quickly without resorting to fad diets or diet pills.

The Self-Hypnosis Diet book will help you to:

- Understand why you gain weight and how to stop it.
- Learn how hypnosis can help you lose weight.
- Start your diet with a deep-state session to condition yourself for the diet plan.
- Lose weight through eight easy steps, including hypnotherapy sessions between each step.

Self-Love and Acceptance

Self-love and acceptance are hard enough, and then there's the added pressure of weight loss. Now you are faced with the difficult decision of how to do it. Weight loss hypnosis is a fast and effective way for women to lose weight quickly and effortlessly.

Extreme rapid weight loss hypnosis not only helps you lose significant amounts of weight in a short period but also helps shift your thinking about food, eating, dieting, and yourself. You learn how to change your relationship with food and lead a healthier life.

These hypnosis sessions can be done at home, at work, or in the privacy of your car. You can listen to a session on audio or video as often as you need. This type of weight loss benefits is easy to see and feel, especially for those who have tried everything else and nothing has worked. It's time for radical changes that will make you feel better about yourself. The old ways didn't work, so trying something new is worth it.

It is easier to stay on track when you know that rewards are waiting for you at the end of each day. You will not have to spend your days feeling frustrated or depressed because the weight loss has gotten out of hand. You will begin to feel better about yourself as you lose weight, and you will start to have more energy as well. There is no other way that you can change your life and start feeling great while at the same time losing weight so quickly.

The key is to change how you look at things, not waste one moment thinking about food or having a nibble here and there. The old ways aren't working, so it's time for drastic changes. You need this weight loss hypnosis done every day because it works too well.

Right now, you are not reaching your full potential, and you need to make a change fast. To lose weight, it's not just about what you eat and how much you exercise. You must also change your habits if you want better results.

The weight loss hypnosis sessions will help overcome the excuses that cause women to fail in their weight loss attempts. They fail because they don't reach their goals fast enough and give up due to their failure to lose weight quickly. If you want to get the most benefit from these sessions, following along with the script is necessary for your success.

You will be guided into a deep state of hypnosis that will help you lose weight quickly and effectively. The sessions are based on the idea that the subconscious mind is what controls our eating habits. The only way to become conscious of this is through hypnosis, so you begin to think differently about food. The only problem with getting too focused on weight loss is that this can cause you to give up faster and more efficiently.

This helps make losing weight a little easier, but it also gives you time back for other things in your life. It's important to remember that as soon as you begin feeling wrong about something, stop, take a look around and see what else can be done...then move on instead of quitting.

The weight loss sessions are designed to make you feel good about yourself and keep you feeling that way. The best way to be motivated is to continue with your weight loss goals is to put the sessions on audio. If you listen to a session in the car on your way home or work, it will reinforce the message and make it easier for you each day.

The weight loss hypnosis script will keep things moving forward and help avoid the ups and downs that many women experience while dieting or trying other programs. It's easy to get discouraged when nothing seems to be happening. This is the worst thing you can do. The sessions will help to keep things positive and keep you feeling good about yourself at all times.

Each day will seem more manageable and better than the last as your weight loss goals become a reality.
Most women feel better about themselves once they lose weight. But there is something about how they carry themselves that makes them look better. The sessions are designed to make you feel fabulous no matter what size you are when you start. It's important not to judge yourself throughout this process and look for ways to be kinder.

You will not be alone on this journey. The weight loss hypnosis sessions are designed to help you feel good about yourself and your situation. It's easy to get distracted, but the weight loss hypnosis sessions keep you focused so that nothing can take that away from you ever again.
The secret to being successful with losing weight is to lose it faster than you can gain it back. Weight loss is a long process and requires a lot of hard work over an extended period. This is something that most people don't have time for, so they use diet pills or other quick fixes because they don't know any better.

The weight loss hypnosis sessions will make you feel good about yourself and help support you in your weight loss efforts. The key is not to feel too bad about yourself. When you are being encouraged by your sessions, it's easier to keep on track and stay committed to sticking with it.
It is easy to see that there will be many different types of weight loss hypnosis sessions available over time, but this one works every single time. This is the best one out there because it has been developed for precisely what you need, and nothing more.

The weight loss hypnosis session will allow you control over your own life again, which we can all appreciate. You will feel like you are in charge of your own life again.
Weight loss hypnosis sessions are the best thing you can do to make significant progress. When some outside force drives you, it's hard to stay on track and focus on what needs to be done. This session is designed for all types of people who need help getting their weight under control, or else they will continue to have the same problems as they get older.

The weight loss hypnosis sessions will not give you anything extra, but they will take away the distractions in your life so that this process can begin and continue with success or failure. You are in charge here, not the outside world. This is something that some people need to realize right off the bat.

It's easy to get distracted when you are trying to lose weight, but the sessions are designed to support you in every way possible. The weight loss hypnosis sessions will help to keep this process moving forward with success and without any distractions.

The best way to lose weight is to do it right away. It's not going to be easy, but if you want something done right, this is the best and most straightforward way that you can go about it.

The real world doesn't care what your scale says or what anyone else thinks about your progress; they want you happy and healthy. It's always a good idea to understand what the real world thinks and how it can help you. There is no better way for you to learn about this than from someone who has been on this journey for many years.

The weight loss hypnosis sessions will help you focus and motivate you to keep on track with it. It's easy to fall off of this diet plan if you are not careful and don't believe in your abilities to make it work for you. The weight loss hypnosis sessions will help motivate and build a great support system to succeed in your goals. The more effort you put into this program, the more successful it will be for you. You have total control over your future with this one. This is a straightforward process that anyone can do, and it will not cost you an arm and a leg to get started. The weight loss hypnosis sessions are here for you right now. Start working hard on this program, and see how much better your life will be short. This is a perfect way to take care of yourself and improve your life.
Weight loss hypnosis sessions will show you how to lose weight faster by using your mind.

You will not have to spend 5,000 dollars when you can learn essential weight loss techniques for the low price of $39. You will understand how everything works and how you can make it happen for yourself. Weight loss hypnosis sessions are a great way to take control of your future and your present and learn what you need to do to reach your goals. This is the most affordable method for helping everyone reach their goals with weight loss hypnosis sessions.

Weight loss hypnosis sessions can help you reach your weight loss goals in record time with a natural approach to achieving your goal weight. With this easy, inexpensive technique, there are no side effects, and you will not need to put anything fake in your body. This weight loss secret works quite well for most people and can help you lose twenty pounds every month.

What is this weight loss secret? It is a good pill that has helped thousands of people lose the extra weight they have been carrying around. It works on the metabolism in your body and causes it to release fat from all the areas of your body that don't need it. The excess fat will be burned off faster because of this unique way of controlling your metabolism. This will provide you with balanced energy in all the energy-producing areas of your body while giving you more power without eating more food than you need.

The best way to lose weight is to take this pill. It has no side effects and will help you gain healthy control over your eating habits. This fat-burning pill should be taken every day for it to be effective. In the meantime, you can start a diet plan that will make you lose weight faster than you would with any other method available today.

You can become as fit as you want to be by taking these pills and following a diet plan carefully, using the instructions that are provided with the drugs. The fat-burning drug works by blocking carbs from being absorbed into your body, leading them away from your stomach and toward your intestines, where they can be eliminated from the body as waste matter.

Benefits of Hypnosis Compared to Restricted Diet

Do you want to lose weight without dieting or exercising? It's possible with hypnosis. Hypnosis can help you lose weight, stop smoking, and reduce stress - plus, it will make you feel better about yourself! In particular, women's bodies are often targeted by hypnosis for weight loss because of the number of physical issues that make overeating a tough habit to break.

Hypnotherapy is a technique in which psychologists put people into an altered state of consciousness to change their unhelpful thoughts and behavior patterns. The most common form is called "hypnotic trance.

With the help of hypnosis, you can eliminate specific conditioned responses to food that cause you to eat when you're not hungry. Hypnosis has been proven to be a successful treatment for weight loss. Medical doctors and psychologists often refer patients who need help losing weight to professional hypnotists.

Our body is a magnificent machine, but sometimes it needs help to release overweight issues. Hypnosis has proven its usefulness in the successful treatment of obesity. It has also been used in treating other conditions such as insomnia, smoking cessation, anxiety and stress management, addiction, and phobias.

Hypnosis is usually used to help people lose weight. Body hypnotists based in Ireland all use the same methods to achieve success. Hypnosis is a safe and easy way to lose weight, and with it, you can have a slim figure without dieting or exercise.

Hypnosis is an excellent tool for controlled weight loss. While overweight people may not be able to stop eating altogether, they can control how much they eat by using hypnosis in the first phases of treatment. This enables the patient to stop eating at mealtimes and learn how to live off calorific intake through snacks that the therapist provides during sessions.

Hypnosis is a safe, effective, and low-cost way to lose weight. Unlike traditional dieting methods, hypnosis involves no strict rules or limitations but instead relies on helping patients use the right mindset to change unhealthy eating habits. It works by putting your mind in a relaxed state where you are more open to suggestions. As a result of being under hypnosis, you make changes in how you think and interpret events that might not otherwise occur. This leads to behavior change when your conscious mind is distracted from the activities that cause you concern by suggestions made to it. This type of therapy is more effective than other approaches in dealing with obesity and anxiety disorders where behavior change may be slow or difficult.

Hypnosis is a natural state of mind, and our body can react to what we believe. It is not necessary to imagine a situation, just relax and think in a certain way. The mind and body are related, so by relaxing; we can achieve what we want with the help of hypnosis.

Hypnosis can be used in many different ways when it comes to losing weight. One of the most popular methods is partial hypnosis. In this type of program, you learn self-hypnosis techniques that will allow you to come out of a hypnotic state on your own.

Hypnotherapy has been proven as an effective treatment for obesity. It has also been used in treating other conditions such as insomnia, smoking cessation, anxiety and stress management, addiction, and phobias. Hypnotherapy is an excellent tool for controlled weight loss. While overweight people may not be able to stop eating altogether, they can control how much they eat by using hypnosis in the first phases of treatment. This enables the patient to stop eating at mealtimes and learn how to live off calorific intake through snacks that the therapist provides during sessions.

Hypnotherapy is a safe, effective, and low-cost way to lose weight. Unlike traditional dieting methods, hypnosis involves no strict rules or limitations but instead relies on helping patients use the right mindset to change unhealthy eating habits. It works by putting your mind in a relaxed state where you are more open to suggestions. As a result of being under hypnosis, you make changes in how you think and interpret events that might not otherwise occur. This leads to behavior change when your conscious mind is distracted from the activities that cause you concern by suggestions made to it. This type of therapy is more effective than other approaches in dealing with obesity and anxiety disorders where behavior change may be slow or difficult.

Hypnotherapy has proven itself over and over again as being an effective treatment for obesity problems. Medical doctors and psychologists often refer patients who need help losing weight to professional hypnotists.

One study looking at weight loss hypnosis found that participants lost more weight than those on either a non-hypnotic diet or cognitive behavioral therapy. Hypnosis may help you learn healthy eating habits, stop eating when truly complete, control emotions surrounding food that cause binge eating, and give you the motivation to begin exercising again.

Hypnotherapy is a natural state of mind, and our body can react to what we believe. It is not necessary to imagine a situation, just relax and think in a certain way. The mind and body are related, so by relaxing; we can achieve what we want with the help of hypnosis.

Hypnotherapy can help you accelerate your weight loss, as it can help you reinvent yourself and not just lose weight.

Every hypnotherapist uses many techniques, but some central concepts are shared among all hypnosis practitioners. One of the most important aspects of hypnosis is its ability to change behavior without side effects naturally. You may think about your eating habits as you would about other activities – that is how we should be considering when it comes to losing weight through hypnosis.

Hypnosis as an Amazing Experience Not Only a Weight Loss Method

What if I told you there was a way to lose weight so fast that it would result in a 30-pound weight loss in just one month? Does that sound too good to be true? Well, it's not. Many people have had incredible success with the rapid weight loss hypnosis for women.

Some say that losing weight fast isn't possible. That it's not healthy, and you'll end up putting the weight right back on. But that's only if you do it the wrong way. Suppose you want to lose weight fast with hypnosis. In that case, all you have to do is follow a strict diet, exercise regularly, and use the right hypnosis techniques to make sure that your body will lose weight quickly without gaining even more fat than before.

How can this be? Well, what happens when you give your body too little food for an extended period? This will force it to go into survival mode to keep itself alive. The body will stop using fat for energy and start to burn muscle tissue. The body has a powerful mechanism that allows it to burn fat so that you don't gain any weight but lose weight.

To keep your body alive, it must use up all of the energy stored in the fat cells for your survival. And once this happens, all of the extra power is used up, and then none of this remains to be used in the future. This means that you'll have no more fat cells to store even more calories at a later time.

The rapid weight loss hypnosis for women uses minimal effort on the part of the user but instead uses your body to do all of the work for you. When you eat less and exercise more, your body will reduce fat stores because it has to naturally. When this happens, you'll begin to burn off excess fat without any additional effort from you on your part.

If that wasn't enough, then there is also a way that you can use hypnosis to help with weight loss and overall health. This is a compelling method for keeping yourself in shape and keeping your weight down by using hypnosis repeatedly throughout the day.

When using hypnosis this way, you'll be able to keep your muscles toned and firm. In turn, this will result in muscle tone that will last a long time after you've stopped using the methods of hypnosis. This is because a certain amount of muscle tone will be built into your system. You can expect to maintain the manners for many years and possibly even decades after you stop using the rapid weight loss hypnosis for women techniques and the other weight loss techniques available, such as working out and keeping a healthy diet.

Not only does rapid weight loss hypnosis for women result in impressive and tangible results, but it also provides many other benefits besides simply helping you to lose more and faster than traditional methods. Some of the other services include improved self-image, reduced depression and anxiety, better energy, improved health, a better outlook on life, and even financial benefits.

Does it sound too good to be true? Well, what if I also told you that rapid weight loss hypnosis for women is quite affordable? It's true. You can get started with your fast weight loss hypnosis for women for only $30. And with regular use of the program and its companion tools, you'll be able to continue getting results month after month without having to pay any additional costs. Best of all, there are no monthly charges or hidden fees once you sign up for the program.

So why is rapid weight loss hypnosis for women so effective? Well, first of all, it's possible to lose double or triple the weight you would lose with traditional methods. Rapid weight loss hypnosis for women lets you tap into and harness the power of your subconscious mind. When your subconscious mind is working with you instead of against you, it can help you make incredible changes that will improve every area of your life.

With rapid weight loss hypnosis for women, you'll be able to tap into the power of hypnosis to take control and make permanent changes in your life through incredibly rapid weight loss. Best of all, you'll be able to do it without any harmful side effects and to help you make these changes; you'll be using a powerful tool that you can use again and again.

You'll also be able to use rapid weight loss hypnosis for women in all the areas of your life that need improvement. Because it's based upon the subconscious mind, it can help in weight loss, self-esteem improvement, behavior change, physical healing, and improved relationships with loved ones and friends. You can even use it in school or at work to improve your grades and performance.

Rapid weight loss hypnosis for women is also incredibly easy to use. All you need is about 30 minutes a day of the program, and if you need to set aside more time, it's beautiful and perfectly acceptable. The program only takes about 15-30 minutes per session, and the rest of the time will be used for applying what you've learned in those sessions to improve your life. There are also optional tools that you can use, such as positive affirmations and journals. These tools are beneficial because they help reinforce the messages delivered by rapid weight loss hypnosis for women.

So why wait any longer to try rapid weight loss hypnosis for women? It's genuinely one of the best investments you can make in your life, and it's completely affordable. It will help you lose weight fast, and it will do it without all the harmful side effects that traditional methods can have. The best part is that there are no hidden costs or monthly charges once you sign up because it's so effective. Rapid weight loss hypnosis for women is a powerful and highly effective way to lose more weight faster than ever before.

Conclusion

Most people have heard something about the importance of diet and exercise when it comes to longevity. But I'm sure you're wondering how much exercise you should do and what type of diet is best.

The link between diet and exercise is a significant one, so we'll start there... Age-related muscle loss can be slowed or halted by maintaining a high level of physical activity or training.

This makes sense for several reasons: muscle tissue burns more calories than fat tissue, so if you're healthier - on the cellular level - it makes sense you'll age better than someone who isn't as healthy.

You see, your muscles are a lot like your fat tissue - they can burn off energy through a process called thermogenesis. The mitochondria in muscle tissue can absorb glucose and fatty acids and use them as fuel. It's been shown that exercise improves mitochondrial energy production.

A recent study showed that when a compound found in green tea was combined with exercise, it boosted glutathione levels in mice's bodies more than exercising alone. Glutathione is our body's most potent antioxidant, and this antioxidant is depleted by exercise.

The bottom line is high levels of physical activity result in increased thermogenesis, energy production, reduced oxidative stress, and improved immune function. As if that wasn't enough, it's also been found that exercise helps optimize your hormones and cuts the risk of cancer.
The most effective way to remain healthy is by getting regular aerobic exercise and weight training.

The type of exercise you choose is not as critical, but it is essential to get plenty of aerobic activity. It's been shown that walking at a leisurely pace every day can add over six years to your life (7). So consider committing to daily walking if you need help forming a regular workout routine.

Why is walking so good for you? This type of exercise has been found to decrease stress levels while boosting your mood and immune system.

When you exercise at a moderate level for 45 minutes, your body releases several brain chemicals that make you feel good. The best news is that these chemicals don't need to be injected to affect your body. You can get the same benefits by simply walking every day.

It's recommended that adults get at least 30 minutes of moderate physical activity on most days (9). We've all heard the benefits of aerobic training: it boosts overall fitness, increases stamina, improves blood pressure, and increases bone density with each passing year. This type of exercise also enhances your immune system and helps keep the weight off.

To get the best cardiovascular workout, try to do some aerobic activity for at least 20 minutes. It's been shown that exercising in short bursts (such as 10 minutes of interval training) results in better cardiovascular fitness than doing a steady-state workout. Not only will you get more out of your training, but you'll also have more energy throughout the day.

If you aren't used to exercising or if you've become inactive, start slow. Work your way up to 30 minutes of aerobic exercise. Some people find that taking a brisk walk for about 20 minutes a day is enough to keep them feeling fit and healthy. Others prefer more prolonged bouts of exercise such as swimming laps or cycling for 45 minutes.

Once you've reached the 20-minute mark, decide whether or not you'd like to increase your workout. To get optimal results, be sure you're exercising at an intensity that makes it difficult to carry on a conversation. This will ensure that your training is practical.

Remember that women might want to train more than men due to age-related muscle loss and other concerns. If you're over 40 years old and haven't exercised in about ten years, begin with a slower exercise (like walking) before moving up to higher intensities. A beginner should start by exercising at about 75% of their maximum capacity. It's essential to avoid injury and ensure your body has time to adjust to the training.

After you've been exercising for a few weeks, you can measure your heart rate at rest and during exercise. Ideally, working out at an intensity of 80% or more of your maximum heart rate will give you the best cardiovascular benefits. You can use a calculator like this to help determine your heart rate at different intensities.

Weight training is also a great way to stay healthy and fit. According to some studies, weight training can improve muscle strength and aerobic capacity even in older adults. It can also help prevent age-related muscle loss, decrease your risk of injury and improve your body's ability to move.

The key is to make weight training a regular part of your fitness routine. A recent study showed that weight training for 24 weeks could increase their strength by about 30% (19). Another investigated the effects of three different exercise programs on older adults with type 2 diabetes mellitus. The results showed that all three exercise programs improved cardio-respiratory fitness and insulin sensitivity.

Studies also show that weight training can help senior citizens become more active, improving blood pressure and glucose levels. Since it works for your major muscle groups, set a goal to work out at least three times per week. You can also check out these muscle-building workouts for seniors for some ideas.

www.ingramcontent.com/pod-product-compliance
Lightning Source LLC
Chambersburg PA
CBHW071529080526
44588CB00011B/1604